LEGISLATIVE PARTICIPATION IN IMPLEMENTATION

LEGISLATIVE PARTICIPATION IN IMPLEMENTATION

Policy Through Politics

Marcus E. Ethridge

PRAEGER

PRAEGER SPECIAL STUDIES • PRAEGER SCIENTIFIC

New York • Philadelphia • Eastbourne, UK
Toronto • Hong Kong • Tokyo • Sydney

Library of Congress Cataloging in Publication Data

Ethridge, Marcus E.
Legislative participation in implementation.

Includes index.
1. Legislative oversight—United States.
2. Legislative power—United States. I. Title.
JK585.E84 1985 328.73'07456 85-6496
ISBN 0-03-004874-5 (alk. paper)

Published in 1985 by Praeger Publishers
CBS Educational and Professional Publishing, a Division of CBS Inc.
521 Fifth Avenue, New York, NY 10175 USA

56789 052 987654321

Printed in the United States of America on acid-free paper

INTERNATIONAL OFFICES

Orders from outside the United States should be sent to the appropriate address listed below. Orders from areas not listed below should be placed through CBS International Publishing, 383 Madison Ave., New York, NY 10175 USA

Australia, New Zealand
Holt Saunders, Pty, Ltd., 9 Waltham St., Artarmon, N.S.W. 2064, Sydney, Australia

Canada
Holt, Rinehart & Winston of Canada, 55 Horner Ave., Toronto, Ontario, Canada M8Z 4X6

Europe, the Middle East, & Africa
Holt Saunders, Ltd., 1 St. Anne's Road, Eastbourne, East Sussex, England BN21 3UN

Japan
Holt Saunders, Ltd., Ichibancho Central Building, 22-1 Ichibancho, 3rd Floor, Chiyodaku, Tokyo, Japan

Hong Kong, Southeast Asia
Holt Saunders Asia, Ltd., 10 Fl, Intercontinental Plaza, 94 Granville Road, Tsim Sha Tsui East, Kowloon, Hong Kong

Manuscript submissions should be sent to the Editorial Director, Praeger Publishers, 521 Fifth Avenue, New York, NY 10175 USA

For Judy

ACKNOWLEDGMENTS

Several individuals have been of great help in my work on this book. Dozens of state administrative and legislative officials took time from their busy schedules to talk with me about difficult and often controversial matters. Their candor and their generosity made possible the research reported here. I also wish to thank John Beasley and William Bates, who, by involving me in the early stages of the Tennessee rule review process, stimulated my interest.

William Boyd, Brett Hawkins, and three anonymous reviewers provided helpful comments on different parts of the manuscript. Their help has been most valuable, although the responsibility for any errors remains mine.

It should be noted that parts of this book have been published in two journal articles. Sections of Chapters 1 and 6 appear in "A Political-Institutional Interpretation of Legislative Oversight Mechanisms and Behavior," Polity, Vol. 17, No. 2 (Winter 1984), reprinted here by permission. Similarly, sections of Chapter 5 were adopted from "Consequences of Legislative Review of Agency Regulations in Three U.S. States," Legislative Studies Quarterly, Vol. 9, No. 1 (February 1984).

Finally, I hope the dedication to my wife indicates how much I appreciated her many hours of painstaking editing, indexing, and re-indexing, and general encouragement.

Marcus Ethridge
Department of Political Science
University of Wisconsin-Milwaukee
Milwaukee, Wisconsin

CONTENTS

INTRODUCTION

On June 23, 1983, the Supreme Court handed down its most important statement on legislative-administrative relations since the New Deal era. Although the case (Immigration and Naturalization Service v. Chadha[1]) dealt with an obscure alien's request for a residence visa, the holding was broadly written to invalidate virtually any official congressional action that did not proceed through the normal law-making process. The enormously popular "political invention" of the legislative veto was held unconstitutional, directly affecting over 200 statutory provisions. As Justice White declared in his forceful dissent, the Chadha decision apparently struck down more congressional statutes than the Court had cumulatively invalidated in its history.[2]

This case, and the widespread negative reaction to it throughout Congress and elsewhere, reveals the extent to which legislative-administrative relations have changed since the Constitution was adopted. Actually, the legislative veto is only one method through which Congress and state legislatures have extended their power over implementation decisions, although it is the most controversial in purely legal terms. An historical view reveals that legislative powers have been increasingly directed toward what were traditionally considered "execution" problems, particularly during the last 50 years. Paradoxically, this development has occurred during a period in which legislative authority to make policy has been increasingly delegated to administrators. The practice of granting broader powers and then instituting a legislative role in implementation has apparently satisfied some political or administrative need or purpose. If so, we can expect that methods for circumventing the recent court decision will be shortly discovered.[3]

This study is an attempt to analyze the origins and impact of the current legislative role in implementation. The issue's importance is indicated by the basic questions it raises about the nature and conditions of the U.S. democratic government. Some interpret the new legislative interest in implementation as a delayed response to the demands (by political analysts and by legislators themselves) for more diligent oversight of administration. Others suggest that legislative involvement in agency and executive affairs is a systemic response to the institutional stresses caused by the policies and exploits of the Johnson and Nixon administrations. Such speculations lead to other, more fundamental queries:

> Will legislative power eventually regain prominence in national politics, as Woodrow Wilson once predicted?
>
> Will legislative scrutiny of bureaucratic decision-making prevent or correct certain improprieties or excessive special interest influence?
>
> Can policy formulation and implementation be effectively integrated through the guidance of powerful and meaningful legislative oversight mechanisms?
>
> Will an expanded legislative role in implementation increase the quality and influence of policy analysis in government decision-making and program evaluation?
>
> Will a stronger legislative presence in administrative decision-making be accompanied by increasing specificity in delegations of legislative authority to agencies?

Answering these questions requires that we study not only the process of legislative participation in implementation, but also its policy implications. Our most basic concerns have to do with the effect of the new legislative role on the effectiveness and representativeness of the policy process. Yet, most studies, even most behavioral ones, have focused almost exclusively on process issues. Significant contributions have been made by these studies, most of which were designed to determine the conditions under which oversight activity is most likely to occur.[4] As a result, we now have some understanding of the committee structures, leadership patterns, party influences, and other factors relevant to the promotion of oversight activity. These studies have helped us understand the process of legislative oversight, but they provide few insights regarding the policy effects of change in the legislative role in implementation.

As the theoretical foundations of the study of oversight became established within a process orientation, research agendas were quickly exhausted. Explanations of the presence or absence of oversight activity could not sustain much scholarly attention. The limiting process view of legislative-administrative relations has persisted, however, because such a perspective is philosophically compatible with mainstream views of U.S. government. The assumption that elected officials should control appointed officials is as well established as any notion in U.S. political thinking. Few would oppose it in abstract terms. Yet, when one begins with this assumption, the possibility that a given instrument of legislative oversight may not be used as a tool for representing the "public interest" becomes quite disturbing. It is much more comfortable to avoid this issue by concentrating on the process questions regarding the presence or absence of oversight activity.

Nonetheless, understanding the contemporary legislative role in implementation requires a deeper study. We must not only ask "Under what conditions does oversight occur?" and "How often does a legislator engage in oversight?" but also "Does oversight effort affect the substance of policy by representing some interests more than others?" and "Does the content of public programs become less consistent when oversight activity is significant?" These are difficult questions, but the importance of the recent changes in our governmental institutions makes it necessary that we attempt to answer them.

The purpose of this book is an ambitious one: to provide a new conceptual framework for evaluating the rapidly changing legislative role in implementation. The original research reported emphasizes regulatory policy on the state level, but the principles and ideas developed are broadly applicable. In this sense, the present effort approaches "legislative behavior" as a general concept, much as John Wahlke et al. approached it in their classic study, The Legislative System.[5] It is hoped that this study will crystallize theoretical questions that transcend the immediate context of its analysis.

The plan of the book is as follows. Chapter 1 provides historical perspective on the legislative role in implementation. The decline of legislative control of policy formulation is traced, beginning with the early period of nearly exclusive legislative control, through periods of clear legislative dominance, and finally to the present period of the "administrative state." The extension of legislative power into the realm of implementation is interpreted as a response both to the decline of power over formulation and to changes in interest group politics.

Chapters 2 and 3 explore incompatible views regarding the policy effect of a stronger legislative role in implementation. The idea that it can facilitate aggressive regulatory policy, an argument closely associated with Theodore Lowi, is developed in Chapter 2. The opposing proposition is discussed in Chapter 3.

Chapter 4 critically examines the assumptions underlying these positions. No attempt is made to determine which is correct, but the strengths and weaknesses of each position are explored. Two subsidiary views are considered in an effort to provide a comprehensive analysis of the major theoretical perspectives on the problem. A detailed examination of these approaches reveals important inconsistencies amenable, in part, to empirical investigation.

Chapter 5 reports the results of data analysis and personal interviews with officials in five states in a parallel format. The specific focus of inquiry involves legislative committee review of formal agency regulations, an innovation that is both enormously important in its practical effects and directly relevant to the theoretical questions addressed in the preceding chapters.

Chapter 6 consolidates the findings from the five state studies. Several propositions are constructed on the basis of these findings, which are suggestive of the policy impact of the new legislative role in implementation. Avenues for future research are indicated.

The final chapter explores the implications of legislative participation in implementation for larger questions regarding U.S. politics. The possibility that the new legislative role is part of a more general adaptation to a "new pluralism" is discussed, and the importance of this development for an assessment of the representativeness of our governmental institutions is considered.

A basic theme of this study is that changes in the legislative role in implementation are not only of importance to the nuts and bolts of public management, but that understanding their effects is essential in any evaluation of the effectiveness and representativeness of U.S. government. This theme was fully appreciated nearly 20 years ago in a provocative essay by Alfred de Grazia. Entitled "Congress: 1989," de Grazia's essay is the imagined text of an address given by the speaker of the House of Representatives on the two hundredth anniversary of the first Congress. After chronicling a wide variety of newly established legislative powers and helpful reforms, this futuristic speech concludes with a positive statement: "[The President] is in his place, and Congress is in its place; and the American Republic retains its place, in turn, as the most stable and powerful republic that the world has ever known."[6] Whether such a pronouncement will be appropriate on that occasion may depend, in large measure, on the changing character of legislative power.

NOTES

1. 77 L.Ed.2d 317.

2. 77 L.Ed.2d 317, at pp. 355ff.

3. Several methods have already been developed. See I. M. Destler, "Dateline Washington: Life After the Veto," Foreign Policy (Fall 1983), pp. 181-86.

4. Two of the most widely cited of these studies are those by John Bibby, "Committee Characteristics and Legislative Oversight of Administration," Midwest Journal of Political Science, Vol. 10 (February 1966), pp. 78-98; and Morris Ogul, Congress Oversees the Bureaucracy (Pittsburgh: University of Pittsburgh Press, 1976).

5. John Wahlke et al., The Legislative System: Explorations in Legislative Behavior (New York: Wiley, 1962).

6. Alfred de Grazia, "Congress: 1989," in Congress: The First Branch, de Grazia, ed. (Washington, D.C.: American Enterprise Institute, 1966), p. 515.

LEGISLATIVE PARTICIPATION IN IMPLEMENTATION

1

THE CHANGING LEGISLATIVE PRESENCE IN POLICY IMPLEMENTATION

The proper form of legislative-administrative interaction is one of the least settled issues in U.S. politics. Perhaps the framers of the Constitution expected it to be so. The principle most directly relevant to legislative-administrative relations, the "separation of powers" doctrine, is easily given to oversimplification and misinterpretation. James Madison went to great lengths to explain that a separation of legislative, executive, and judicial functions did not mean that the three branches of government must be "totally separate and distinct"; it was not necessary that they have no "partial agency in, or no control over, the acts of each other."[1] However, while the proper extent of this "partial agency" may have been clear to Madison, generations of legislators, administrators, and executives have reached widely disparate conclusions.

The Constitution does provide some guidance on the correct balance of legislative and executive power, of course, and several important judicial opinions have helped to shape that balance.[2] Nonetheless, as with most basic elements of U.S. politics, legislative-administrative relations have varied widely within established legal precepts. The legislative role has, at different times, been one of complete control of administration, indirect control, and virtually no control at all. However, variations in legislative-administrative relations are not merely the result of idiosyncratic decisions by prominent politicians or of shifts in judicial opinions. Legislative involvement in implementation has changed in accordance with changes in the larger political environment. An understanding of legislative-administrative interaction thus depends more on an appreciation of the ways in which it is affected by political developments and the ways it affects policy than on a reading of constitutional provisions and common law doctrine.

Describing the current legislative role in the policy process is difficult because some mechanisms and powers that legislators use to influence administrative decisions ("sunset" legislation, for example) appear to be more important as symbols or in their relation to legal concepts than in their real political impact. Nonetheless, it is clear that a fundamental change has occurred during recent decades. Both Congress and many state legislatures have enacted a wide variety of new mechanisms establishing their independent authority (and often the authority of their committees) over administrative actions taken to implement public policies. The new legislative role is active, forceful, controversial, and involved in implementation activities more than ever before, at both the state and national levels.

Table 1.1 lists the most prominent control mechanisms recently enacted by state legislatures and by Congress. There are important differences among the legislative veto, committee rule review, and the other mechanisms (to be discussed in detail later), but they are similar in that they create new powers and opportunities for legislators to alter implementation decisions without recourse to the whole law-making process. This feature distinguishes these mechanisms from the investigations, hearings, and required reporting normally considered part of the oversight process. Joseph Harris defines the latter as

> review after the fact. . . . inquiries about policies that are or have been in effect, investigations of past administrative actions, and the calling of executive officers to account for their financial transactions.[3]

Normally, improper or inefficient administrative practices uncovered by oversight activities are corrected through statutory revision. In contrast, legislative participation in implementation implies formal, binding action (often by

Table 1.1 Major Forms of Legislative Participation in Implementation

	Legislative Veto	Committee Rule Review	Sunset	State Legislative Control of Federal Grants
Basic Description	Specific administrative or executive decisions or actions made contingent upon approval by one or both houses or by a specified committee during a certain period	All proposed administrative regulations submitted to legislative committee for review prior to promulgation	Agency authorizations subject to periodic renewal and evaluation by legislative committee or staff	Federal grants to state agencies subject to approval and appropriation by legislative resolution or committee decision
Extent of Adoption	Primarily federal; over 300 provisions have been enacted, more than 175 since 1969; held unconstitutional, 1983	Primarily adopted by state legislatures; currently adopted in 35 states, 33 since 1968	Essentially a state innovation; currently adopted in 41 states, all since 1974	Some grant control power now in 34 states; nearly all established or strengthened recently

Source: Compiled by the author.

a committee or one house) with regard to proposed actions or decisions for which the authority was delegated to administrators. Whatever terminology is used, it is clear that the establishment and rapid proliferation of these mechanisms has substantially altered legislative-administrative relations. Consequently, the ways in which citizens, public advocate organizations, client groups, and other interests influence the policy process have been fundamentally changed.

Several explanations have been offered for the recent expansion of legislative participation in implementation, all of which are plausible in the context of contemporary U.S. politics. For example, James Sundquist has written a thoughtful treatise on recent changes in congressional power in which he interprets the adoption of new control mechanisms as part of a general reaction to the excesses of executive power. The new assertiveness arose, according to Sundquist, "out of anger, and anxiety, and public pressure and contempt."[4] Widespread opposition to Nixon's Watergate-related exploits, and to the foreign policy decisions of both Johnson and Nixon, led members of Congress from both parties to advocate new reforms reasserting congressional authority. Public opinion polls taken during the 1970s revealed that the average citizen wanted Congress to be more powerful; a 1974 poll found that 87 percent of the respondents felt that the balance among the branches of government had been upset, and most perceived this to be a result of excessive executive power.[5]

Congressional rhetoric adds support to the conclusion that the new legislative role is, in large part, a reaction to executive encroachment and its effect on public opinion. One representative brought the matter down to fundamentals: "The issue is who makes the laws in this country . . .? The House will come down on the side of the people who are fed up with Washington bureaucrats running their lives."[6] Another heatedly informed Nixon: "Our warning is that the Congress will not stand by idly as the President reaches for more and more power."[7] Reading these and a multitude of similar statements certainly gives one the impression that recent changes in legislative power are simply efforts to reestablish the position of legislative institutions where it has been eroded by executive excesses and encroachment. Such a reestablishment is naturally defended by reference to the most basic constitutional and democratic principles.

Other interpretations have also been offered. The expanding legislative presence in implementation has been seen as a response to increasing resource scarcity. Legislators are said to be more interested in meaningful policy evaluation when fiscal conditions require program reductions.[8] At least one observer has contended that "altruistic" legislators concerned about good government have been more frequently elected in recent years, and that the presence of even a few of them could account for expanding oversight powers and activities.[9] On a more general level, some argue that public dissatisfaction with government regulation and spending programs has grown dramatically, leading legislators to become more concerned about bureaucratic supervision.[10]

These explanations have an undeniable intuitive appeal. Executive excesses, fiscal constraint, and generalized dissatisfaction with regulatory policy are all widely perceived contemporary political phenomena, and it is reasonable to expect that legislatures would respond to them by significantly enlarging their presence in implementation decisions. In short, there are good reasons to argue that oversight has become more important to the political system and more actively demanded by public opinion. These factors thus provide satisfying explanations for the new legislative role in implementation.

However, conclusions from mainstream research on legislative oversight make it difficult to accept these interpretations. Scores of studies have emphasized that oversight activity depends on its <u>political profitability</u> as perceived by individual legislators, and that it does not occur primarily as a response to the objective needs of the system.[11] Political success normally requires that the legislator devote scarce time and resources to constituent service and legislation, and that powerful "policy subsystems" be allowed to operate freely. A legislator's political position is thus best protected by avoiding oversight activities.

Legislators rarely work against their political self-interest even for party or ideology; that they do so because of an abstract concern for executive excess or fiscal responsibility seems highly improbable. And yet, if it is true that oversight normally produces a political net loss for most legislators, the above interpretations of the new legislative role imply that legislators regularly make such sacrifices. A better explanation is needed, one which is consistent with widely confirmed views of legislator motivations and political incentives.

It is contended here that if the new mechanisms of bureaucratic supervision have actually created a new legislative presence in agency decision-making, then oversight activity--at least certain varieties of it--must have become politically rational. This view assumes that the patterns of influence among agencies, organized interests, and legislators have been substantially altered, making oversight profitable where it has not been profitable before.

The argument suggested here is developed as follows. The enormous growth of public interest advocacy has affected administrative behavior, campaign strategies, and policy implementation; it may have also changed legislative-administrative relations. It is clear that while public interest advocacy is not strictly a recent phenomenon, the growing political influence of consumer, environmental, and other public interest groups during the past two decades has vastly increased its importance.[12] Analysts now argue that public advocacy has produced a "profound transformation" in agency operation and that it has become "one of the most distinctive features of American administration."[13] Such groups change the political setting not only because the causes they support are relatively new, but because they effectively oppose interests that were previously unopposed in their efforts to control administrative decision-making. Effective participation by these groups has contributed to a new polarization of forces acting in policy implementation.[14]

A conspicuous indication of the extent to which influence patterns have changed can be seen in the now widespread support for elaborate, "judicialized" administrative procedures. Thirty years ago hearing procedures, due process requirements, and other reforms associated with the Administrative Procedure Act were expected to enable regulated groups to block agency implementation of aggressive regulatory policies and programs.[15] Few analysts hold such opinions today, however, primarily because public advocate groups have developed organizational styles and capacities that make the elaborate procedures of modern administrative decision-making quite useful to them. The "judicial-type" character of contemporary bureaucracy is thus supported and profitably used both by the regulated and by the public advocate supporters of aggressive, public-oriented regulation.[16]

The increasing effectiveness of public advocates in influencing administrative decision-making alters legislators' calculations of the political costs and benefits of oversight activity. Quite simply, public advocate organizations disturb the linkages between client or regulated groups and many government bureaus--indeed, this is the explicit purpose of most public advocate groups.[17] Interests that had been largely unopposed in their relations with administrators now regularly encounter effective public advocate groups pressing for administrative decisions contrary to their preferences. Before public advocacy became politically important, oversight was avoided because it could interfere with the cooperative and mutually beneficial relations among legislators, interest groups, and agencies. Effective public advocacy has disrupted policy subsystems, leading previously unopposed interests to turn to legislators with demands that they modify or reverse agency decisions made at the behest of public advocacy organizations.

While the emergence of public advocacy has created new problems for previously unopposed interests, it has also created new opportunities for legislators. The policy process itself has become increasingly polarized and difficult (one observer termed the last two decades the "age of protest"[18]), since incompatible demands are effectively exerted at nearly all stages of policy formulation and implementation. Of course, intense conflict has always been a feature of the policy process, but traditional influence patterns tended to moderate it when regulatory programs and policies reached the implementation stage. Reformist-oriented groups concentrated their efforts on legislation, while the interests subject to the resulting regulatory mandates would eventually work closely with the implementing agencies. Marver Bernstein, Murray Edelman, Theodore Lowi, and several others developed classic theoretical explanations for both the stability of this syndrome and the ineffective regulatory policy associated with it.[19] By challenging these established patterns, public advocacy has created a situation in which legislators are more frequently asked to intervene in implementation decisions. Figure 1.1 is a diagrammatic representation of this idea.

This interpretation suggests that the legislative presence in implementation should grow in conjunction with the rise of public advocacy, and that is precisely what the data show. Figure 1.2 charts the years in which the major national public interest lobbies were established and

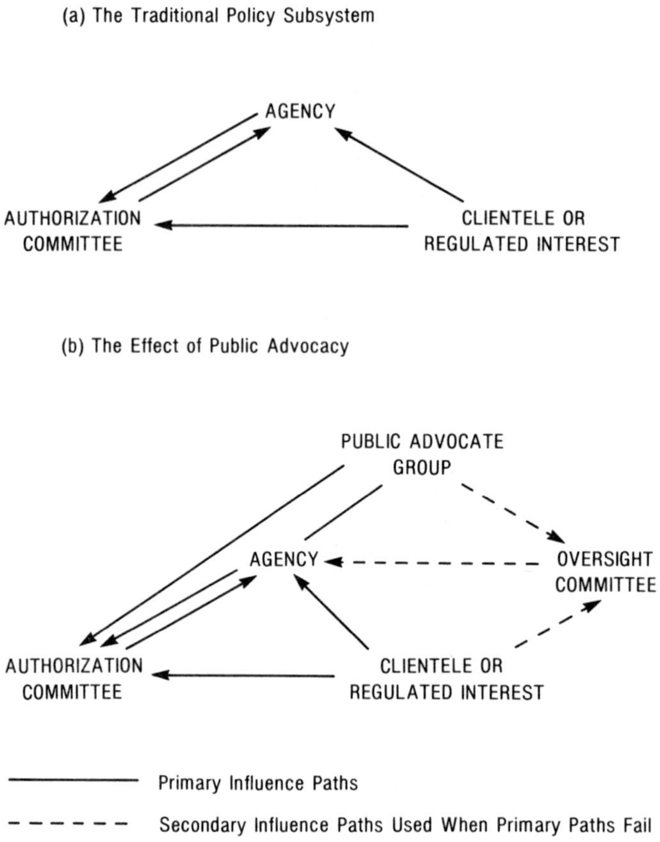

Figure 1.1 The Effect of Public Advocacy on Traditional Legislative-Administrative Relations

the expansion of legislative veto and rule review machinery in Congress and among state legislatures. The close association is striking.

A wealth of examples illustrates how effective public advocacy can create new demands for oversight. Used car dealers complained to Congress about proposed Federal Trade Commission regulations, developed with the support of consumer groups, which would have required them to disclose information about known defects in their cars.[20] In Tennessee, a liquor retailers' association successfully demanded a legislative committee veto when the Alcoholic Beverage Commission (supported by a consumer lobby) attempted to repeal certain anticompetitive restrictions on advertising. Alternatively, legislative participation may occur in response to public advocate pressure when such groups fail to hold sway in agency decision-making. A Wisconsin legislative committee upheld an agency regulation that limited premiums charged to consumers for credit life insurance, a proposal that was intensely opposed by the insurance industry.[21] As a result of these and many similar cases, legislators of every stripe have strong incentives to establish and use mechanisms giving them selective, formal leverage in agency implementation decisions.

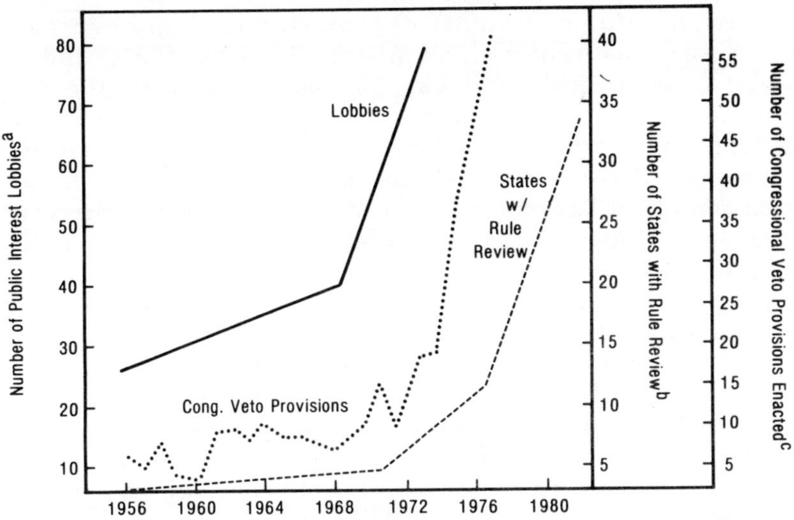

[a]Information on the growth of public advocacy is from Jeffrey M. Berry, Lobbying for the People (Princeton: Princeton University Press, 1977). Comparable figures not available after 1972.

[b]Compiled from statute search and from Keith Hamm and Roby Robertson, "New Methods of State Legislative Oversight," paper delivered at the 1979 Annual Meeting of the American Political Science Association, Washington, August 31-September 3, 1979.

[c]Compiled from Lawrence C. Dodd and Richard L. Schott, Congress and the Administrative State (New York: Wiley, 1979), pp. 231-232.

Figure 1.2 The Concurrent Spread of Public Interest Advocacy and New Legislative Oversight Mechanisms

However, despite the fact that these mechanisms are frequently used, and despite the legal rhetoric employed to defend them, there is no reason to assume they will lead to systematic monitoring of agency behavior to ensure efficiency and administrative adherence to legislative purposes (that is, "oversight"). The new legislative presence in implementation has not been created primarily to correct instances of executive or administrative noncompliance with statutory intent (although it can occasionally be used for such a purpose), but to facilitate legislative responses to salient demands for changes in implementation decisions regardless of whether or not current implementation is consistent with applicable statutes or previously stated legislative intent.

This interpretation helps to explain some apparent paradoxes. If we assume that the mechanisms are created primarily to respond to uncoordinated demands and not to achieve meaningful oversight, the existence of greater oversight activity (as reported by Aberbach, Rosenthal, and Sundquist, among others[22]) can be reconciled with the continuing failure of legislators to achieve systematic monitoring and consistent evaluation of administrative activity. Quite simply, these new oversight mechanisms do not herald a "resurgence" of legislative power, but a basic redirection of influence. This conclusion is well expressed in a recent judicial opinion in which it was argued that the current legislative role is no longer directed toward achieving "oversight with an eye to statutory revision," but to create a legislative presence in day-to-day administrative decisions.[23] That this role is necessarily applied selectively does not diminish its importance in the policy process as a politically relevant avenue of influence, although it explains why the new role can never achieve the "continuous watchfulness" ostensibly intended by most oversight reforms. Responding to occasional political demands for changes in implementation decisions by exercising, for instance, a committee veto of agency action does not require as much legislative capacity as true oversight would require. The political incentives created by the contemporary interest group climate, along with the limits on legislative time and resources, make it likely that the new mechanisms will function in actuality as selective political tools instead of methods to achieve oversight.

Relatedly, the puzzling imbalance between the breadth of delegation and the growth of oversight activity is also accounted for by this interpretation. If it is true that effective oversight is not the real purpose of these reforms, it follows that the legislators adopting them are not necessarily interested in overall limits on administrative authority. Only legislators sincerely concerned about maintaining legislative control of the policy process would favor both oversight reforms and meaningful restrictions on delegated authority. In this connection, it is interesting to note that, in fact, contemporary administrators are given increasingly broad delegations of legislative authority. Some have vehemently protested about the position in which overbroad delegation places them. A recent undersecretary of the Department of Health and Human Services (then Health, Education, and Welfare) resigned his position after criticizing Congress for mandating "a program to protect the rights of the handicapped with but 'one line' of statutory language." The purpose of the intentional ambiguity was, according to the undersecretary, avoidance of legislative "conflict over details," and he was understandably frustrated when the Congress opposed whatever decisions he reached regarding those details.[24]

Such frustrations are apparently quite common. In fact, two observers have concluded that there has been a conspicuous increase in "symbolic" legislation during the last few years, indicated by the fact that "careful scrutiny and understanding of the substantive provisions of [legislation] is often sacrificed in the focus on goals and intentions."[25] Implementation problems are encountered when important questions are not resolved in legislation, questions that inevitably demand some kind of legislative action. Nonetheless, it is apparently easier to build legislative coalitions when troublesome substantive issues are not resolved in policy formulation.[26]

Thus, changes in patterns of political influence have placed legislators in the rather anomalous position of establishing new oversight powers while at the same time delegating broader authority to administrators. Agency discretion continues to grow despite the various reforms ostensibly instituted to control it. The anomaly exists simply because the same political pressures that inhibit resolution of substantive policy issues in legislation (thereby making delegation more politically attractive) also produce demands for selective legislative involvement in administrative decisions. These concurrent developments--the decline of legislative resolution of policy formulation issues and the expanding legislative role in implementation--raise important questions about the representativeness and the effectiveness of the policy process.

The distinctiveness of contemporary legislative-administrative relations can best be appreciated from an historical perspective. A brief survey of the changing legislative role in budgeting and in controlling administrative discretion reveals how present circumstances have evolved in response to conflicts among political demands, legislative capabilities, and deep-seated ideas about government machinery.

LEGISLATIVE CONTROL THROUGH THE BUDGETARY PROCESS

The changing legislative role in budgeting reveals how political incentives, legislative capacities, and public policies determine the nature of legislative influence in implementation. Legislative capacities were large relative to the task of formulating budget documents for the government during the first half of the last century. Early budgets were consequently assembled by the Congress with extreme specificity, allowing administrators little flexibility in normal management decisions.[27] Literally every government expenditure was set forth as a line item. Congress pursued such a strategy in order to maximize popular control over government actions and because, from an accountant's perspective, the system was formally quite "accountable."

Early problems with this system illustrated the difficulties created by comprehensive legislative control of administrative discretion. Detailed itemization of government expenditures in budget enactments was not administratively sound. Alexander Hamilton described some of its more unfortunate consequences:

> The exigencies of public service are often so variable that a public agent would often find himself full-handed for one purpose, empty-handed for another, and if forbidden to make a transfer, not only the service would suffer, but an opportunity, with very strong temptation, would be given to traffic with public money for private gain; while the business of government would be stagnated by the injudicious and absurd impediments of an overdriven caution.[28]

The practical necessities of administrative efficiency and flexibility in an expanding government made it difficult to maintain this extremely specific congressional itemization of the budget. Ironically, control capacity itself began to deteriorate as a result of the strategy because agencies began to use "deficiency requests" when needs changed during the budget cycle. Administrators found they had overestimated their needs in some areas while underestimating them in others, and the strictness of itemization prohibited most shifting of funds. The emergence of deficiency requests as an answer to excessive itemization actually led to reduced legislative influence since the requests were, of necessity, almost always honored.[29] Thus, instead of having firm and systematic legislative control of spending through a precise budget document, the actual budgets of many agencies were changed several times during the year, with relatively little congressional deliberation.

The absence of systematic budgetary direction would not soon be corrected by legislative efforts. By the late 1800s the budget was divided into well over a dozen annual funding bills, and no single committee had jurisdiction over more than half of them. Although the structure was illogical, Joseph Harris explained that this "fiscal crazy quilt" evolved for clear political reasons. The House Appropriations Committee, in which much of the budgetary responsibility had traditionally been focused, had become politically unpopular because of its broad power. The legislative response--a general decentralization of budgetary authority in both the House and Senate--allowed many important committees to exert influence over certain programs, thus satisfying political needs at the expense of coordination.[30]

The clarity of the political logic did not redeem the resulting inefficiencies and irresponsibilities. A spending heyday ensued as each committee supported the spending plans of other committees so that its proposals would be accepted. Rapidly growing revenues made it possible to absorb the increases, but sensitive observers realized that the system could not long endure. Planning was made particularly difficult by the uncertain nature of decision-making. Deficiency requests were still referred to the Appropriations Committee even when they were issued by departments whose budgets were originally written in other committees.[31]

State legislatures were operating on a smaller scale during this period, but they were also experiencing the difficult transition from highly specific itemization to more general budget formulation. The typical state budget system was characterized by a minimum of gubernatorial involvement; each agency made its own appropriations requests directly to the legislature.[32] The resulting lack of coordination led to the same patterns of waste and inefficiency that plagued the national legislature.

State governments consequently were ill-equipped to manage the increasing scope of public policy demanded by their citizens. The budget process itself became riddled with impropriety. Lacking the higher visibility of the Congress, state assemblies became notorious centers of corruption as wealthy interests made good use of the generally unsupervised access opportunities available.[33] Even aside from the ubiquitous problem of graft, it quickly became recognized that sound financial policy was impossible when the estimates of funding needs by state agencies were not revised by a central office.[34]

Congress and many state legislatures were ready to establish an executive budget shortly after World War I. The Budget and Accounting Act of 1921 created the Bureau of the Budget and authorized the president to draft a comprehensive budget proposal. Similar reforms were adopted on the state level, although more gradually. Governors have full responsibility for preparing the budget in nearly all the states now, and they have at least some influence over the budget in those states without executive budgets. It is interesting to note that the majority of the states without full gubernatorial control of budget preparation are southern states, which are characterized by a relatively low level of government spending and relatively small bureaucracies.[35] The establishment of the executive budget has followed the expansion of administrative activity, being less popular among the states in which such activity is less developed.

However, the Federal Budget and Accounting Act illustrates that an executive budget can coexist with active legislative involvement. In addition to the establishment of the executive budget, the congressional reorganization accompanying the act concentrated congressional budget evaluation in the appropriations committees. Some have argued that the effects of this unification of congressional responsibility more than offset any loss of budget formulation power to the executive. The Budget and Accounting Act was clearly not an attempt to make the budget into a purely executive institution.[36]

A classic essay by Edward Banfield, written some three decades after the act was passed, supports these ideas.[37] In much the same way that the budgetary process had been criticized at the turn of the century, he complained that the proper role of Congress "is not to formulate the budget, . . . but to supply the pattern of key value judgments around which the budget is built." Banfield argued that continuing legislative involvement in specific aspects of budget formulation inevitably created a fragmented process in which effective planning was impossible.[38]

It is interesting to note that Banfield's criticisms, with which many contemporary administrators would undoubtedly agree, were written during a time of widely perceived legislative decline. Unprecedented government growth during the 1950s and 1960s gradually made the executive budget more powerful. The advent of advanced policy analytic techniques and the necessity for long-term planning of major projects with important technological or scientific components further diminished legislative management of the public budget. The budget reforms of the 1970s (creation of the Congressional Budget Office [CBO], changing the fiscal year to October 1, and impoundment controls) were an attempt to strengthen the congressional role, but few contemporary legislators expect a return to the pre-1921 legislative dominance of the budgetary process.[39] The creation of the CBO and the delay of the fiscal year starting date made Congress better able to evaluate the president's budget, and the limits on presidential impoundment authority decrease his unilateral power over later changes. However, the fact that the congressional review of the budget has not often been completed by October 1 indicates that legislative capacities are still severely strained. Moreover, the initial successes of the Reagan administration in its budget policies reveal the great potential of executive control of the overall shape and direction of the budget.

The current legislative-administrative balance in the budgetary process is thus based on a difficult and contentious division of labor that reveals the importance of legislative interests and incentives. Both state legislatures and Congress found it difficult to maintain comprehensive control of budgeting, and most budget authorizations became more general as a result. The need for a "superior revision" eventually led to the executive budget, long after the need for it was obvious. Nonetheless, the budgetary process remains significantly open to legislative influence over selected specific concerns. Legislators have not been content to supply only "key value judgments," as Banfield once hoped. The loss of control over formulation was accompanied by a continuing legislative interest in controlling isolated details.[40]

LEGISLATIVE POWER AND ADMINISTRATIVE DISCRETION

Legislative control of administrative discretion has followed a similar pattern, although much rhetoric has served to obscure it. During the very first years of American government, administrators had no administrative discretion at all, not only because of the extreme specificity of budgetary formulation, but also because, for a brief period, legislative committees directly administered government activities.[41] It became quickly accepted, however, that departments headed by a single appointee constituted a better solution to administrative needs. Since the Constitution was ratified, there has thus been a trend toward weakening legislative control and expanding executive and administrative power.[42]

The first legislative response to growing administrative discretion was simply to ignore it. As long as administrative decisions did not create controversy and did not contravene legislative intent, legislators allowed a measure of discretion to exist without acknowledging its legal status. A similar attitude was even more easily maintained at the state level. The principle of administrative discretion was therefore not developed or legitimized either in common law or in popular political thinking.

The reluctance to recognize administrative discretion on matters of policy was a necessary solution to a basic problem of democratic theory. Since bureaucrats are not elected, no government in which they are given independent authority over policy decisions can be truly democratic. They have some kind of authority, of course, a fact that has made many observers uneasy. A solution persuasive to some involved a conceptual distinction between "administrative" and "political" authority. Woodrow Wilson's classic essay was primarily a plea for expanded study of administration as a separate field of applied research, but it is most often remembered as the foundation of the initial academic perspective on public administration. All governments must perform two functions, Wilson explained, politics and administration.[43] Democratic responsibility was intact as long as the power given to bureaucrats was only administrative in character. Wilson felt that the administrative process was so distinctive that traditional political theories were largely irrelevant to administrative problems; hence his suggestion that there is no necessary difference between administration in a democracy and administration in a dictatorship.

A philosophical basis was thus established for legislative dominance over the major issues of public policy and for a limited kind of administrative power. However, despite Wilson's argument regarding proper legislative and administrative roles, legislative power over policy formulation would gradually be diminished and progressively applied more selectively. Just as in the budgetary process, political incentives would work against the direction of legislative influence toward broad policy concerns. Wilson's argument was eventually discredited as a result.

The New Deal era made it impossible to continue ignoring the reality of administrative discretion for two reasons. First, the sheer quantity of government programs, especially in areas previously untouched by public intervention, made the abstract notion of a politics/administration dichotomy rather hollow and unconvincing. Agencies were beginning to make policy for regulation of child labor, support of the arts and humanities, and a variety of other efforts designed to stimulate economic recovery. Second, in addition to the expanded scope of government activity, many of the statutes passed in the 1930s included explicit delegations of clearly legislative power, making administrative discretion a legal reality. Congress delegated authority for everything from the establishment of a "code of fair competition" for the poultry industry (one of the few delegations eventually held unconstitutional by the Supreme Court[44]) to authority to set standards for the quality of imported tea. Even casual observers could see that administrative power consisted of much more than the authority to carry out the decisions of elected officials.

When the New Deal demolished the last vestiges of the politics/administration dichotomy, basic political values were unsettled. The system would have to adapt its institutions so that mainstream political traditions could be preserved. Of course, the controversy was not entirely philosophical, since many groups opposed bureaucratic expansion for explicit reasons of self-interest. Conservatives, particularly those in the legal community, advocated reforms that would presumably constrain administrative powers that were being used to create and enforce a variety of labor restrictions and other actions opposed by business groups. The combination of concrete political interest and sincere convictions about constitutional values challenged by administrative discretion produced important governmental changes in the post-New Deal years.[45] However, these changes were not capable of reversing the trend toward legislative decline and growing administrative power, and it can even be argued that they accelerated it.

It is useful to distinguish analytically two elements in the New Deal era opposition to expanding administrative discretion. Although they were closely associated in practice, the guiding philosophies of the two elements were different, and consequently, the reforms they engendered were different. One portion of the opposition was primarily legal in its orientation; for lack of a better term we will designate the other as "political." Both perspectives were predominantly conservative with regard to policy matters, but positions on issues of principle and constitutional interpretation were not merely useful vehicles for conservative ideologues. The great debates over the propriety of administrative discretion during the 1930s revealed that this period was, indeed, a time in which the most fundamental ideas regarding the relationships among U.S. political institutions were dramatically changing.

The legal component was largely tied to a literal interpretation of article 1, section 1 of the Constitution: "All legislative power shall be vested in a Congress of the United States." New Deal policies that involved a direct grant of law-making authority to appointed bureaucrats were, from this perspective, quite understandably seen as violating the most basic elements of the Constitution. Many programs also included delegations of judicial authority, enabling administrators to levy fines and other penalties against private parties judged by the agency to be in violation of administrative regulations.

The initial legal reaction to these developments was a concerted opposition to delegation itself, a strategy that would not prove long-lived.[46] After delegation was upheld as constitutionally sound, the struggle focused on the role of courts in reviewing administrative decisions and on reform of administrative procedures. The enactment of the federal Administrative Procedure Act (APA) of 1946 (and 49 state APAs beginning in the 1940s) constituted the most important expression of this legal concern with the problem of administrative discretion. Continuing controversies over the scope of agency power and its control through judicial review and procedural restrictions eventually became the primary concerns of the rapidly growing field of administrative law.

Paradoxically, while the APA was initially an expression of antibureaucratic sentiment, it may have indirectly strengthened bureaucratic authority. Through its institutionalization of a variety of formal procedural requirements, administrative decisions have acquired greater visibility, legitimacy, and force. The APA's provisions for open and well-publicized formal hearings have facilitated the development of citizen participation and the growth of agency linkages to a wide variety of organized interests. The groups that are successful in using the new administrative procedures naturally favor broad grants of power and discretion to the agencies they influence. Moreover, as mentioned earlier, regulated groups, client groups, and proregulatory public advocate groups have all found the elaborate, time-consuming "reformed" procedures quite helpful during recent years. Thus, instead of limiting administrative discretion, these reforms may have led to an easier expansion of administrative power.[47]

The APA satisfied many of the legal objections to administrative discretion, but it did not directly address the basis of the political opposition to administrative power. The institution of procedural requirements could only moderate a portion of the widespread concern regarding administrative discretion; as long as administrators followed procedures mandated by law and did not violate constitutional and legal rights, their decisions were still autonomous, subject only to statutory change. Thus, a second reform statute, the Legislative Reorganization Act (LRA), was also adopted in 1946.

It had become clear by this time that effective legislative involvement in administrative activity was impossible as long as legislative power was severely disintegrated. The act reduced the number of standing committees in both the House and Senate, and it structured the remaining committees to create a roughly parallel system. Jurisdictional disputes were to be minimized by more clearly specified committee boundaries.[48] The LRA of 1946 was an attempt to make the Congress more "rational" and "streamlined" in its operation so that effective control of administrative discretion could be achieved.

Moreover, the LRA explicitly addressed the issue of legislative oversight. Standing committees were directed to exercise "continuous watchfulness" over the activities of the agencies under their jurisdiction. Dodd and Schott explain that the process of oversight was allocated by the act to three types of legislative committees: "(1) the Appropriations Committees would have control of agency budget requests, (2) the Government Operations Committees would review administrative structure and procedures, and (3) the authorization committees would review program implementation."[49] The act thus specified how oversight was supposed to proceed in addition to asserting the authority for it.

Legislative efforts to control administrative discretion have emphasized various forms of oversight activity since the 1940s. In a narrow, formal sense, these oversight reforms may be interpreted as tools for controlling the administrative discretion that must, for practical reasons, be delegated. They certainly have not been effective for that purpose, however; one representative complained that the LRA was nothing more than "patchwork, improvisation, and tinkering."[50] As a reform intended to reassert congressional authority over administrators, the LRA appears rather half-hearted.

In fact, this reform statute, like the APA, may have contributed to the continued growth of administrative discretion. Dodd and Schott argue that a primary consequence of the act was increased independence of committee chairs, leading to further deterioration of coordinated party control.[51] Access opportunities for organized interests were multiplied by these developments. The idea of oversight to maintain the integrity of legislative purpose was therefore not promoted, as agencies and committees worked together with ever-increasing autonomy. It should not be surprising that the LRA of 1946 did not succeed in slowing the expansion of administrative discretion.

Both the APA and the LRA, as well as many of the subsequent oversight reforms, were defended as ways to maintain basic democratic values where they were perceived to be threatened by bureaucratic expansion, but both have also arguably strengthened administrative power. The continual weakening of legislative power and the consistent ineffectiveness of oversight activity make it difficult to view these failures as merely the result of poor draftsmanship or of lapses in leadership. The growth of administrative discretion is more likely the result of political factors.

THE EVOLUTION OF LEGISLATIVE PARTICIPATION IN POLICY IMPLEMENTATION

Mechanisms establishing a legislative presence in implementation existed in a few contexts before the World War II era, but, as discussed earlier, the last few decades have witnessed a great increase in statutory provisions giving legislators and their committees authority over implementation decisions. The mechanisms vary considerably in terms of their legal effects, but they are similar in two important particulars. First, they reflect an apparent acceptance of administrative discretion. Limiting discretion through budgetary itemization or by narrowing delegated authority is no longer seen as a realistic approach to the problem of controlling bureaucracy. And, more important, a return to nondelegation would arguably be contrary to legislators' self-interest. Second, legislative participation mechanisms enable legislators to act <u>after</u> administrative decisions have been made.

H. Lee Watson refers to these new measures as "extra-legislative Congressional controls," in that they place "upon members of Congress a responsibility to take future action which is not a part of the ordinarily recognized legislative process."[52] The original and most common form of this participation (on the congressional level) is the legislative or committee veto, incorporated in scores of statutory enactments, all of which are now apparently unconstitutional. Under these provisions, executive officials made certain decisions, but the legislature (or a designated committee) was empowered to disapprove the decisions after they are proposed, usually during a specified time period. The growth and recent demise of this mechanism makes for an interesting bit of legal history.

One of the first examples of a legislative veto provision was incorporated into the Senate version of the League of Nations Treaty in 1919. It would have allowed the Congress to declare U.S. withdrawal from the League by concurrent resolution. When the idea was attacked as unconstitutional because it omitted executive participation from the ultimate decision, it was argued that "Congress has the power to base termination of membership on any contingency it cared to choose, and enactment of a concurrent resolution could be taken as such a contingency."[53] The issue became moot when the Senate voted against League membership, but the concept nonetheless took firm root.

Committees were gradually expanding their powers during this period. The traditional functions, investigating and reporting, were obvious adjuncts to legislation. The new duties represented a departure from these activities in that they permitted committees to make independent decisions with immediate impact. The first applications of extralegislative committee powers were not of fundamental substantive importance; for example, committees in both houses of Congress acquired authority to select sites for monuments in the capital and to manage some aspects of government printing.[54] Although these powers were relatively insignificant, they illustrate the ease with which legislators have transcended purely legislative activities.

Partially as a result of presidential opposition, the application of a legislative veto through a concurrent resolution did not expand rapidly until the 1940s. The 1939 Reorganization Act marked the beginning of the extensive use of the mechanism. This act provided for the rejection of presidential proposals for reorganization acts by concurrent resolution, as have most reorganization acts passed since that time. (A concurrent resolution does not require a presidential signature, presumably because it is not expected to be used for any "legislative" purpose.[55]) It is noteworthy that Roosevelt had actively opposed such a provision in earlier acts, signing the 1939 bill only because of the need for immediate action.[56]

The rationale for the legislative veto reveals much about the development of legislative control of administration. It was argued that delegation of "unlimited" legislative power was unacceptable to democratic theory, but the detailed nature of increasingly complex policies and programs made active legislative resolution of all formulation problems impractical. Writing in the first volume of Public Administration Review, two observers saw the legislative veto provision in the reorganization act as a way around the tension between democratic control and efficiency:

> The legislative veto of acts of the executive has pointed to an answer to the dilemma between the demand for no further delegation of unlimited power and the need for legislative action upon matters whose controversial details threaten to prevent any action at all.[57]

Thus, the idea was established quite early that, when legislators cannot resolve all the details of a program or plan, they can delegate the authority to do so to administrators, while reserving their right to disapprove decisions after they have been proposed or made. The fact that this later legislative action does not include executive participation was considered acceptable, since the legislators were merely deferring a decision that they clearly had a right to make.

The committee veto is more controversial in that it allows a single committee to annul administrative proposals. The rationale is identical to that of the legislative veto, however. The committee finds it difficult to resolve all aspects of a legislative problem, and thus it recommends an authorization that provides for later committee action on administrative decisions that prove objectionable. Among the best examples of this kind of legislation are the military construction bills passed during the Truman administration. After vetoing an identical bill a few months earlier, Truman signed a 1951 bill that allowed the Armed Services Committees to veto any military real estate transactions in excess of $25,000. The urgent need for the legislation forced Truman to sign the bill with the veto provision included.[58]

Despite active opposition by Eisenhower, Johnson, Nixon, Ford, and Carter, many legislative veto provisions in several forms were enacted during the subsequent 25 years. The acts involved everything from post office bases to small project reclamations to reobligation of economic assistance and even the alteration of forest boundaries in publicly owned forests.[59] Legislative vetoes have also been included in acts regulating arms sales, presidential impoundment actions, and decisions covered by the War Powers Act. The use of the device became even more popular and wide-ranging in the 1970s, and recent trends suggest that the interest in using it is still significant. Presidents of both parties and vastly different political persuasions have, in principle, opposed this growth of legislative influence; but in the interest of obtaining new legislation the provisions were generally accepted, frequently without comment.[60] The legislative veto thus became an institutionalized control mechanism.

The Chadha Decision

The Supreme Court handed down a remarkably broad opinion on June 23, 1983, which held all legislative veto provisions unconstitutional.[61] Ironically, the case arose not from a major regulatory policy issue but out of an alien student's request for permanent residence status. Jagdish Rai Chadha remained in the United States for some time after his student visa had expired and was thus deportable. He received a notice from the Immigration and Naturalization Service (INS) to show cause why he should not be deported. Chadha applied for a suspension of deportation and appeared at a formal hearing in accordance with applicable statutes. An Immigration judge concluded that Chadha satisfied the standards for a suspension of deportation (he had been in the country for at least seven years, he was of good moral character, and he could show that deportation would cause hardship), and the suspension was so ordered.

In December 1975, some 18 months after the suspension was ordered, the chairman of the House Judiciary Committee's Subcommittee on Immigration, Citizenship, and International Law introduced a resolution opposing the granting of permanent residence to six aliens, including Chadha. The subcommittee had reviewed 340 cases, and they concluded that the "hardship" requirement was not satisfied for these six. Chadha claimed that the veto by House resolution was unconstitutional in a hearing before the INS. The INS refused to rule on the constitutionality issue and ordered him deported in accordance with the House resolution.

Chadha then filed a petition for review in the Court of Appeals, an appeal in which the INS joined. The court held the veto provision unconstitutional, and was upheld by the Supreme Court when the decision was appealed by the House and Senate.[62] The Supreme Court's reasoning is worth considering in some detail because it reveals how far the legislative role in implementation has strayed from a strict construction of constitutional principles and because the opinion may suggest some avenues for circumvention or moderation of the prohibition against extralegislative power. The specific grounds for holding the legislative veto unconstitutional were the separation of powers doctrine implicit in the presentment clause, and bicameralism.

In writing the majority opinion, Chief Justice Burger made reference to concerns expressed by the framers in 1787. The purpose of the presentment clause was, according to Madison, to establish an effective limit on congressional power. The legislative branch was considered the most dangerous; in fact, Burger reported that Madison and others were concerned that the new Congress would attempt to evade the president's influence by simply labeling an action a "resolution" rather than a bill. The Chadha decision rejects any legislative measure that does not incorporate presentment to the president as being squarely contrary to the intent of the framers.[63]

The bicameralism issue in Chadha is based on very similar reasoning. Any act of the Congress must be supported by both houses (except those specifically designated as requiring only one or the other: Senate confirmation of treaties and appointments, House impeachment decisions, and Senate conviction decisions). The fact that passage by both houses is difficult and cumbersome is not only the generally expected result, but, according to Burger, this was the explicit intention of the framers. They structured legislative activity so that "the legislative power of the federal government would be exercised in accordance with a single, finely wrought, and exhaustively considered procedure."[64]

It is revealing that the Chadha opinion is so adamant in refusing to temper its relatively strict reading of constitutional provisions with considerations regarding the needs and realities of modern administration. Justice White argued for such an approach, contending that the legislative veto was an extremely useful "political invention" that enabled Congress to create agencies, to endow them with legislative authority, and yet to secure their accountability. As he saw it, the removal of the veto left Congress with a Hobson's choice:

> [Congress must either] refrain from delegating the necessary authority, leaving itself a hopeless task of writing laws with the requisite specificity to cover endless special circumstances, or, in the alternative, to abdicate its law-making function to the executive branch and the independent agencies.[65]

Justice White contended that the Court should have followed the reasoning expressed in the dissenting opinion in FTC v. Ruberoid Co.,[66] in which it was suggested that the bureaucracy's existence as a fourth branch of government made a strict adherence to the separation of powers doctrine inappropriate.

The majority opinion acknowledged that the legislative veto may be a beneficial invention but it was, nonetheless, unconstitutional. In fact, Burger went a long way toward admitting that the holding created the dilemma White described: "Congress must abide by its delegation of authority . . . until that delegation is legislatively altered or revoked."[67] The creation of a large administrative establishment thus does not alter constitutional limits on legislative influence, according to Chadha. Moreover, perhaps to reveal that there was no confusion on the issue, Burger wrote: "Convenience and necessity are not the primary objectives--or the hallmarks--of democratic government."[68]

The long-term effects of this decision are difficult to predict. Perhaps, as some analysts hope, Congress will begin to formulate policy with more precision, as was done in the Clean Air Act, for example.[69] Sufficient narrowing of administrative discretion could obviate the need for legislative veto authority. However, it is virtually certain that a comprehensive, precise approach to legislation is beyond the capacities of Congress and, as discussed earlier, contrary to important political incentives. Some predict that the absence of veto authority will require Congress to adopt the role Banfield once thought appropriate: setting the basic "value judgments" that guide policy implementation.[70]

The problem with both of these predictions is that they give insufficient weight to the political incentives driving legislative behavior. The veto authority did not become popular only because certain legal doctrines were inaccurately interpreted, but because it improved the ability of legislators to represent. Whether the representation facilitated by this and other extralegislative powers is democratically sound is unclear; the research reported in this volume is largely designed to answer this question. Yet, if real political forces created the veto, it is likely that the judicial invalidation will be circumvented. There are already indications that informal methods will be designed to allow legislators to exercise control through actions short of legislation. (One approach that will probably be popular is the "fast track" procedure that authorizes the president to submit a draft bill under binding rules requiring Congress to vote for or against it without amendment within 90 days.[71]) In any case, the key to understanding future developments with regard to the congressional role in implementation is a complete appreciation of the relevant political motives.

State Legislatures and Implementation

Legislative involvement in implementation on the state level has also expanded since the 1940s, and although the same mechanisms have not been employed, the general development of legislative power has been strikingly similar to the congressional changes outlined above. State legislatures established new mechanisms to control administrative activities in response to the widening scope of governmental activity and the accompanying political changes during the last two decades. The primary difference between the federal and state approaches is that congressional influence in implementation has been expanded through statutes pertaining to individual agencies or programs, while state legislatures have adopted generic statutes establishing certain kinds of legislative influence over all state agencies.

The earliest form of systematic state legislative participation in implementation was described in an excellent case study by Glendon Schubert, the title of which plays on the resulting confusion of governmental functions: "Legislative Adjudication of Administrative Legislation."[72] Generally speaking, the mechanism Schubert discussed granted a joint committee of the Michigan legislature the authority to disapprove and suspend administrative regulations. Although action by the entire legislature could rescind committee disapprovals, the committee was empowered to act independently. Approximately two-thirds of the states now have some form of legislative committee rule review, although there are important differences among the statutes.[73]

The ostensible rationale for this kind of legislative control is quite straightforward. State legislatures have long been frustrated by administrative actions that contradict or ignore explicit legislative mandates. For example, agency officials in one state adopted regulations that contained provisions from bills actually defeated by the legislature.[74] Similar practices have reportedly occurred in other states. Apparently, when an agency fails to obtain passage of a bill it supports, some officials have felt free to adopt important provisions by regulation. Even if such blatant abuses are uncommon, it is understandable that state legislators feel that additional controls are needed.

Clearly, the establishment of legislative committee rule review is logical and reasonable when viewed from a purely legal perspective. Many supporters of the mechanism are members of the legal profession who see the problem as one of merely determining when agencies have exceeded the scope of authority delegated to them or when they have contradicted legislative intent. Many judicial opinions are based on records of obscure committee hearings on enabling legislation or on speeches by legislators; committee rule review would provide a relatively concrete guide to legislative intent by giving legislators an opportunity to rule directly on a particular agency action. Some argue that the mechanism operates as a generally neutral device, similar in practice to the usually perfunctory review that regulations are given by state attorneys-general who determine whether each set of agency proposals is promulgated by someone with proper statutory authority and in accordance with proper procedures.

In some states, this picture may be accurate.[75] If the committee becomes institutionalized as a neutral tool designed to ensure procedural and legal regularity, substantive policy issues may remain within the realm of enabling legislation and appropriate administrative discretion. A strong professional staff of attorneys can help to establish such a neutral stance. However, even a superficial understanding of legislative committee behavior suggests that a committee empowered to suspend agency regulations will usually not be satisfied to determine simply whether an agency's proposed actions "fall within the four corners" of the applicable statutory authority.

The available evidence indicates that most committee members have felt quite unrestrained in their willingness to go beyond technical issues when performing this review. When rule review committees function in this manner, interesting questions are raised regarding the representativeness of the committee's actions. It is possible, for example, that a legislator who has opposed the original legislation authorizing a set of regulations would be able to use his committee position to block or delay the regulations implementing the legislation, even if they are legally sound and faithful to legislative intent. Interest groups are certainly given another point at which to exert influence; if a group fails to get its way when legislation is being considered in an authorization committee or in the whole assembly or when regulations are promulgated in administrative hearings, the rule review committee provides an additional, separate access point through which to oppose a program. The policy consequences of this mechanism will be considered later. At this juncture, it is only necessary to point out that legislative committee rule review creates a special channel through which some legislators can participate in implementation decisions not only for oversight purposes, but also to respond to salient political demands expressed after policy reaches the implementation stage. Consequently, of all the mechanisms creating a new legislative presence in implementation, committee rule review has the most direct relevance to the theoretical discussion presented at the beginning of the chapter.

The sunset acts currently popular among state legislatures are supported by the same antibureaucratic rhetoric often used to support the other devices. In their simplest form, sunset laws merely authorize a periodic review of agencies and their programs by requiring positive approval by the legislature in order for the agency to continue to operate. Although legislatures have always had the authority to terminate programs, the sunset provision requires a formal, periodic review of government activities.[76] It institutionalizes a critical evaluation of agency activity by legislators and is thus in formal terms the closest approximation to true oversight. At present, about four-fifths of the states have adopted some kind of sunset legislation.

Greater legislative control of administrative activities is expected to result from the establishment of sunset acts, although the effect of sunset on the substance or direction of policy is a matter of some contention. It is clear, however, that the mechanisms have formally expanded the role of the legislature in evaluating the implementation of government policies and programs.

This is not to say that sunset legislation has created the kind of "continuous watchfulness" that was envisioned by the Legislative Reorganization Act of 1946. The most striking finding in nearly all studies of sunset acts is that the evaluation they produce is limited and usually insignificant. Systematic monitoring and assessment of bureaucratic decisions and actions do not occur for the same reasons that effective oversight has not been achieved through other reforms: the time and staff resources required to accomplish a comprehensive review are too great and the political incentives too weak. Nonetheless, the mechanism of sunset review may have an important impact in certain cases by uncovering controversial agency actions or practices.[77]

State legislatures have expanded other powers over administration as well, the most recent of which is legislative control of federal grants to state agencies. This mechanism raises basic questions about federalism (for example: Is a state required to implement "national" programs?), but the rationale is similar to the ideas behind the other mechanisms. State agencies routinely implement policies and programs that are funded by federal agencies. Although the state agencies are presumably "creatures of the state legislature," these federally funded programs often involve policy decisions of a highly controversial and substantive nature. State legislators quite properly feel they are losing control over major aspects of state policy.[78] The new controls often give a committee the authority to disapprove grant applications and to appropriate the funds that are granted.

PROBLEMS AND PARADOXES--THE NEW LEGISLATIVE ROLE IN IMPLEMENTATION

The history of the legislative role in implementation has been one of numerous attempts to accommodate changing political incentives and changing public policies. Although legislative influence has experienced various cycles of expansion and decline, a fairly consistent trend can be discerned that describes the changes during the first 150 years of U.S. government. Despite forceful protestations by conservative legal scholars, and contrary to considerable legislative rhetoric, legislative control became consistently less comprehensive as administrative power expanded. After a brief period of administration by congressional committee, legislative control was diminished by: declining specificity in budget itemization; the emergence of the executive budget; the rejection of the nondelegation doctrine; and the increasing breadth of delegated authority. Unprofitable resolution of major policy questions was avoided by an increasing emphasis on certain isolated details of budget formulation (to the apparent frustration of many planners), and, as programs became larger and more complex, legislators even delegated many details to agency decision-making. Practical administrative needs coupled with subsystem pressures for a measure of autonomy tended to diminish legislative control over the substance of policy. These developments help to explain why some analysts contend that much recent legislative output is symbolic.

The increasing political intractability of policy-formulation conflicts has been accompanied by new demands for selective legislative participation in implementation. The mechanisms adopted to facilitate authoritative responses to the demands have been seen by some analysts as indications of a generalized legislative resurgence, but there are good reasons to discount such a view. The fact that these mechanisms have been applied selectively, and most often in cases in which policy subsystems have been challenged or disrupted, suggests that their establishment is not a function of increased legislative concern for fiscal responsibility or even for the integrity of legislative mandates.

The current legislative interest in implementation can thus be interpreted as the culmination of a long-term development instead of a reaction to recent events. The resolution of major policy controversies--theoretically the main purpose of legislative authority--has become unprofitable for most legislators. As a result, new ways to avoid this task have been devised: initially dividing budget authority so that major allocation issues would not be addressed; increasing the independence of committees and subcommittees; delegating ever-broader authority to bureaus. The new legislative role in implementation, despite its forceful, authoritative nature, should not be expected to reverse these trends.

However, significant impacts are possible, the policy consequences of which are uncertain. While the most important control mechanisms have been adopted in response to pressure from interests recently displaced or effectively opposed by public advocates, the mechanisms may be used in a number of ways. Legislators participating in implementation may ultimately neutralize each other, since some applications of the new powers will be in support of regulated or client groups while others will support opposing interests. Under this assumption, legislative participation would be no more or no less representative than legislative influence in general. In other words, its cumulative policy impact would be neutral, although it could affect administrative efficiency and the continuity of programs being implemented.

However, it is also possible that inherent features of the new legislative role in implementation make it nonneutral with regard to the substance of policy. There are good reasons for arguing that, contrary to certain expectations, legislators will use their new powers over implementation primarily to correct overly "permissive" administrative decisions. Equally sound arguments can be made in support of the opposite conclusion; legislative participation may be disproportionately applied to weaken "aggressive" administrative decisions. The policy consequences of the new legislative role depend on the extent to which it is cumulatively neutral or, alternatively, the extent to which one of these other propositions is accurate. The next two chapters explore the theoretical foundations for the idea that legislative participation is, in practice, a nonneutral form of influence.

NOTES

1. James Madison, "Federalist #47," in Alexander Hamilton, James Madison, and John Jay, The Federalist Papers, ed. Charles A. Beard (Garden City, N.Y.: Doubleday, 1948), p. 12.

2. An excellent examination of the legal evolution of current legislative-administrative relations, with coverage

of pivotal judicial opinions, can be found in H. Lee Watson, "Congress Steps Out: A Look at Congressional Control of the Executive," California Law Review, Vol. 63 (1975), pp. 983-1094.

3. Joseph Harris, Congressional Control of Administration (Washington, D.C.: Brookings, 1964), p. 9.

4. James Sundquist, The Decline and Resurgence of Congress (Washington, D.C.: Brookings, 1981), p. 6.

5. Ibid.

6. Ibid., p. 353.

7. Ibid., p. 6.

8. Joel D. Aberbach, "Changes in Congressional Oversight," American Behavioral Scientist, Vol. 22 (May-June 1979), p. 499.

9. Alan Rosenthal, "Legislative Behavior and Legislative Oversight," Legislative Studies Quarterly, Vol. 6 (February 1981), pp. 130-131.

10. This theme is well articulated by John H. Sheridan, "Can Congress Control the Regulators?" Industry Week, Vol. 188 (March 29, 1976), pp. 20-27.

11. Perhaps the best statements of this idea are those of Morris Ogul, Congress Oversees the Bureaucracy (Pittsburgh: University of Pittsburgh Press, 1976), p. 202; and Morris Fiorina, "Congressional Control of the Bureaucracy: A Mismatch of Incentives and Capabilities," in Congress Reconsidered, 2d ed., Lawrence Dodd and Bruce Oppenheimer, eds. (Washington, D.C.: Congressional Quarterly Press, 1981), pp. 343-346.

12. Jeffrey M. Berry, Lobbying for the People (Princeton: Princeton University Press, 1977), pp. 33-35.

13. Walter A. Rosenbaum, "The Paradoxes of Public Participation," Administration and Society, Vol. 8 (November 1976), p. 355; and D. Stephen Cupps, "Emerging Problems of Citizen Participation," Public Administration Review, Vol. 37 (September-October 1977), p. 478.

14. Cupps, pp. 483-484.

15. Herbert Simon, Donald Smithburg, and Victor Thompson, Public Administration (New York: Knopf, 1950), p. 521.

16. Peter Woll, "Administrative Law in the Seventies," Public Administration Review, Vol. 32 (September-October 1972), p. 558.

17. See James Q. Wilson, Political Organizations (New York: Basic Books, 1973), pp. 292-296; and Cupps, pp. 483-484.

18. Lawrence D. Dodd, "Congress, the Constitution, and the Crisis of Legitimation," in Congress Reconsidered, 2d ed., Lawrence Dodd and Bruce Oppenheimer, eds. (Washington, D.C.: Congressional Quarterly Press, 1981), pp. 400-401.

19. Marver Bernstein, Regulating Business by Independent Commission (Princeton: Princeton University Press, 1955); Murray Edelman, The Symbolic Uses of Politics (Champaign-Urbana: University of Illinois Press, 1964); and Theodore Lowi, The End of Liberalism, 2d ed. (New York: Norton, 1979).

20. This action was reported in the Washington Post, May 27, 1982, p. C1.

21. The state examples are discussed in more detail in Chapter 5. It should be noted that California is atypical in the context of the present discussion in that it has powerful public interest lobbies but no committee rule review powers. Perhaps this important deviant case suggests that when the strength of public advocacy reaches some theshold level, committee rule review no longer provides an effective means for opposing public advocate groups. Ideas regarding the complex connections between interest group politics and legislative participation in implementation are discussed in detail in Chapter 7.

22. See notes 4, 8, and 9.

23. Consumer Energy Council of America v. Federal Energy Regulatory Commission, Court of Appeals, D.C. Circuit, 673 F. 2d 425 (1982).

24. Sundquist, p. 320.

25. Timothy J. Conlan and Steven L. Abrams, "Federal Intergovernmental Regulation: Symbolic Politics in the New Congress," Intergovernmental Perspective, Vol. 7 (Summer 1981), pp. 19-26.

26. Ibid., p. 23.

27. Harris, p. 50.

28. Quoted in ibid., p. 50.

29. Ibid., p. 52.

30. Ibid., pp. 53-54.

31. Ibid., pp. 54-55.

32. Leslie Lipson, The American Governor: From Figurehead to Leader (Chicago: University of Chicago Press, 1939), p. 38.

33. Wilder Crane, Jr., and Meredith W. Watts, Jr., State Legislative Systems (Englewood Cliffs, N.J.: Prentice-Hall, 1968), p. 4.

34. Lipson, p. 70.

35. Joseph A. Schlesinger, "The Politics of the Executive," in Politics in the American States, 2d ed., Herbert Jacob and Kenneth N. Vines, eds. (Boston: Little, Brown, 1971), p. 230.

36. Lawrence C. Dodd and Richard L. Schott, Congress and the Administrative State (New York: Wiley, 1979), pp. 78-80.

37. Edward C. Banfield, "Congress and the Budget: A Planner's Criticism," American Political Science Review, Vol. 43 (December 1949), pp. 1217-1228.

38. Ibid., p. 1219.

39. Allen Schick, "Congress and the 'Details' of Administration," Public Administration Review, Vol. 36 (September-October 1976), p. 523.

40. Ibid., p. 526.

41. Cornelius P. Cotter, "Legislative Oversight," in Congress: The First Branch, Alfred de Grazia, ed. (Washington, D.C.: American Enterprise Institute, 1966), p. 27.

42. Ibid.

43. Woodrow Wilson, "The Study of Administration," Political Science Quarterly, Vol. 2 (June 1887), pp. 197-222.

44. Schecter Poultry Corp. v. U.S., 295 U.S. 495 (1935).

45. For an excellent discussion of the political and legal aspects of this controversy as seen from an historical perspective, see Alpheus Thomas Mason, The Supreme Court from Taft to Burger (Baton Rouge: Louisiana State University Press, 1979), ch. 3.

46. Ibid., p. 101.

47. In addition to legitimizing administrative action, administrative procedure reform also may improve the power position of administrators by making the administrative process more intricately "legalistic." Guy Benveniste argues along these lines in Regulation and Planning (San Francisco: Boyd and Fraser, 1981), p. 92.

48. Dodd and Schott, p. 86.

49. Ibid., p. 87.

50. Ibid., p. 89.

51. Ibid., p. 91.

52. Watson, p. 988.

53. Ibid., p. 1004.

54. Ibid., p. 1007.

55. Cornelius P. Cotter and J. Malcolm Smith, "Administrative Accountability to Congress: The Concurrent

Resolution," Western Political Quarterly, Vol. 9 (1956), pp. 957-958.

56. Watson, p. 1013.

57. John D. Millett and Lindsay Rogers, "The Legislative Veto and the Reorganization Act of 1939," Public Administration Review, Vol. 1 (Autumn 1940), p. 178.

58. Watson, p. 1020.

59. The appendix in Watson's essay contains a useful list of these provisions.

60. Watson, pp. 1017-1027.

61. Immigration and Naturalization Service v. Jagdish Rai Chadha, 77 L.Ed.2d 317.

62. The House and Senate joined the suit when it was argued before the Court of Appeals.

63. Chadha, p. 342.

64. Ibid., p. 344.

65. Ibid., p. 355.

66. 343 U.S. 470 (1952).

67. Chadha, p. 347.

68. Ibid., p. 340.

69. For a good analysis of the specificity of the Clean Air Act, and of the difficulties it encountered in implementation, see Daniel Mazmanian and Paul Sabatier, Implementation and Public Policy (Glenview, Ill.: Scott, Foresman, 1983), pp. 86-137.

70. A good discussion of these possibilities in the context of foreign policy decision-making is contained in I. M. Destler, "Dateline Washington: Life After the Veto," Foreign Policy (Fall 1983), pp. 181-186.

71. Ibid.

72. Glendon Schubert, "Legislative Adjudication of Administrative Legislation," Journal of Public Law, Vol. 7 (1958), pp. 135-161.

73. For a useful survey of current state rule review mechanisms, see R. Craig Williamson, "Legislative Review of Administrative Rules and Regulations," paper presented at the Annual Meeting of the Southern Political Science Association, Memphis, November 5-7, 1981.

74. See Edwin L. Jackson, "Legislative Review of Administrative Rules and Regulations," paper presented at the Annual Meeting of the Southern Legislative Conference, Charleston, S.C., July 1977.

75. See the brief description of Florida's system in Chapter 6.

76. Benjamin Shimberg, "The Sunset Approach: The Key to Regulatory Reform?" State Government, Vol. 49 (Summer 1976), pp. 140-147.

77. Lowi expresses such an optimistic view in The End of Liberalism, p. 310.

78. James E. Skok, "Federal Funds and State Legislatures: Executive-Legislative Conflict in State Government," Public Administration Review, Vol. 40 (November-December 1980), p. 563.

2

LEGISLATIVE PARTICIPATION AS A FACILITATOR OF REGULATORY AGGRESSIVENESS

> Quite as important as legislation is Congressional oversight of administration.[1]

> Democratic ideology requires control of administrative action by elected representatives of the people.[2]

> The proper office of a representative assembly is to watch and control the government.[3]

> The legitimacy of the bureaucracy is conditioned on the assumption that the legislature . . . is setting the criteria, inquiring whether they are met, and providing for corrective action.[4]

> Control of administration is one of the most important functions of legislative bodies in all modern democracies.[5]

> An efficient and orderly Congressional oversight system will compel the regulatory agencies to respond more vigorously to changing needs.[6]

The preceding quotations are drawn from the writings of a wide variety of commentators, including politicians and scholars from many points on the ideological spectrum and covering a period of over 100 years. It appears that the principle of legislative control of administration is virtually unassailable. No one is willing to assert that appointed bureaucrats should be free from supervision by the "elected representatives of the people." Quite simply, a straightforward approach to democratic theory requires that effective controls over administrators be in the hands of the citizenry.

One might well find it difficult to explain the generally contentious nature of the issue of legislative oversight throughout much of the nation's history in light of the apparent unanimity regarding its place in governmental machinery. However, if we leave the abstract world of normative democratic theorizing and consider actual applications of legislative control mechanisms, we will discover that the authors of the remarks cited above are in serious disagreement. Like other issues thought to be largely matters of constitutional principle, arguments over the proper form of legislative oversight are closely linked to assumptions and preferences regarding its impact on the substance of public policy.

Most of the scholarly analysis in support of the new legislative role in implementation is based on the assumption that the structural changes instituted to achieve it will lead to more aggressive, comprehensive, and effective regulatory policy. This chapter explores the arguments behind this proposition. The analysis is drawn from a broad range of literature, some of which directly addresses the issues raised by various mechanisms of legislative control of bureaucracy. However, a considerable portion of the literature discussed is not explicitly concerned with these mechanisms but develops more general notions that are, nonetheless, germane to our concerns. A critical examination of the literature will inform the subsequent construction of research hypotheses.

LEGISLATIVE POWER AND PLURALISM

The idea that a stronger legislative role in implementation will lead to more aggressive regulation is based on an assumption that more precise and effective legislative control mechanisms, by their essential nature, inevitably work to counteract "subsystem politics." The argument is simple, elegant, and, to some, quite persuasive.

If it is established both that the fragmentation caused by delegated legislative authority allows regulated interests to control regulators, and that the reassertion of the rule of law through strengthened, centralized legislative control mechanisms will reverse the fragmentation, then one may reach the conclusion that an expanded legislative role will lead to more aggressive advocacy of the public interest in regulatory policy implementation. The two parts of this argument are independent and should therefore be discussed separately.

The idea that policy is largely determined and implemented under the direction of informal subsystems is one of the most durable notions among students of U.S. politics. Building upon the growing appreciation, initiated by Arthur Bentley, of extralegal and extraconstitutional political factors, Ernest Griffith was among the first to assert such a view of the policy process. In 1939 he explained that

> one cannot live in Washington for long without being conscious that it has whirlpools or centers of activity focusing on particular problems. . . . It is my opinion that ordinarily the relationship among these men--legislators, administrators, lobbyists, scholars--who are interested in a common problem is a much more real relationship than the relationship between congressmen generally or between administrators generally.[7]

The neat delineation of policy-making authority to Congress and of execution authority to administrative agencies presupposed by legal-institutional analysis was quickly considered hopelessly simplistic after political scientists began studying actual behavior. The <u>real</u> patterns of political responsibility involved close connections among interest groups, legislative committees, and agencies or bureaus working in the same policy area. According to many analysts, the subsystems have become generally autonomous and quite stable.[8]

The development of policy subsystems is usually attributed to a few basic characteristics of U.S. party politics and legislative behavior. The normally low party disciple both in state legislatures and Congress makes it impossible to force legislators to support a coherent program or plan. The rise of "committee government" and the increasing importance of subcommittees compound the problem. Consequently, except when public opinion is unusually strong on a particular issue, the subsystems are free to adopt policies that are highly inconsistent or contradictory and beneficial to only an identifiable, organized private interest. Perhaps the most glaring example of this phenomenon is the juxtaposition of tobacco subsidies and government campaigns against smoking. Most observers consider such a situation patently irrational, but the subsystem theory makes the political logic underlying it quite clear.

The low visibility of most public policy decisions and programs and the weakness of party government permit the subsystems to operate with considerable latitude. As Leiper Freeman explained:

> Policy-making is often left to essentially subordinate units of the Administration and Congress. Similarly, the parties often leave issue politics to interest groups. In this sense, such subunits of the political setting, encouraged by diffused power and functional specialization of political expertise, tend to enjoy a relatively wide range of autonomy. Policy tends to be "farmed out."[9]

Thus, the most important sources of power in U.S. government are not designated by constitutional provision or institutional structure, but are developed through informal linkages among governmental and nongovernmental actors in relatively distinct issue areas.

There are positive explanations for the existence of policy subsystems; they are not only the result of the absence of party government and centralized legislative authority. As government became an ever-stronger force in private life, the idea of being a legislator became more prestigious and attractive. Congressional careers became longer, and most members now expect to be repeatedly reelected. Since the Civil Service System added stability to many administrative positions, personal relationships between legislators and bureaucrats interested in a certain set of programs or policies developed easily. The overall professionalization of government thereby has helped to institutionalize subsystem linkages.

Moreover, the absence of central political authority necessitates the development of subsystems. Administrators and legislators cannot rely on some central authority to provide the necessary support to enable them to achieve their policy objectives. Consequently, both seek effective allies in each other and in private organizations affected by their efforts. Subsystem politics is, in part, a result of this search for political power. Norton Long's analysis is instructive here:

> It is clear that the American system of politics does not generate enough power at any focal point of leadership to provide the conditions for an even partially successful divorce of politics from administration. Subordinates cannot depend on the formal chain of command to deliver enough political power to permit them to do their jobs. Accordingly they must supplement the resources available through the hierarchy with those they can muster on their own, or accept the consequences in frustration.[10]

As bureaucrats develop independent sources of political support in subsystems of private organizations and small groups of legislators, the fragmentation of public authority is further accelerated.

There is considerable divergence of opinion regarding the policy consequences of subsystem politics. Analysts have argued along several very different lines: the emergence of subsystem politics has allegedly made the policy process more representative,[11] slower,[12] more rational,[13] and difficult to plan.[14] Some clearly approve of its effects while others do not. Yet, within the realm of regulatory policy, there is a general consensus that policy subsystems lead to moderate, instead of aggressive, regulatory policy implementation. (There is not, of course, wide agreement on whether moderate regulation is in the public interest.)

One of the most frequently cited statements of this view is Marver Bernstein's Regulating Business by Independent Commission.[15] His overall conclusion--that regulatory commissions initially act aggressively but inevitably become tools of the regulated after reform movements expire--has been endorsed by many politicians and scholars. Perhaps the best example of this kind of development is the Interstate Commerce Commission (ICC). Established in 1887 as the result of a political crusade by early consumer advocates, the ICC was ostensibly intended to protect consumers from unfair pricing policies by railroads with natural monopolies. Yet, it quickly became apparent that the commission had become an advocate for the railroads. President Cleveland's attorney-general sent the following revealing message to a leading railroad executive:

> The Commission, as its functions have now been limited by the courts, is, or can be made, of great use to the railroads. It satisfies the popular clamor for a Government supervision of railroads, at the same time that the supervision is almost entirely nominal. Further, the older such a commission gets to be, the more inclined it will be found to take the business and railroad view of things.[16]

Not surprisingly, the most important effect of ICC's early policies was to increase the railroad rates that effective competition had held down.[17]

Bernstein's point is that this development is not unusual or the result of isolated corruption. The "independent" nature of the commissions releases them from political control, insuring that they will become captured by the regulated and make policies contrary to the public interest. While the special structure of the independent commissions may make these effects of pluralism especially severe, others extend the argument to all agencies, contending that the typical fragmentation of power leads to close regulator-regulated linkages regardless of their formal-legal relationship with the chief executive. As noted in the previous chapter, this more general argument is associated with Theodore Lowi's *The End of Liberalism*, one of the most influential books of recent years.[18]

It is not necessary to review all or even most of Lowi's elaborate polemic. The essential points are that political authority is extremely fragmented in the modern "liberal" state, and that public policies are therefore designed and implemented under the direction of salient interest groups. Regulatory policies are largely a restatement of industry standards (as in the case of some OSHA standards), or are wholly arbitrary and unpredictable, making planning impossible.[19] The removal of policymaking from the centers of public authority (a primary consequence of excessive delegation) makes it unlikely that public objectives will hold sway over private interests in policy implementation.

Although analysts often disagree about the virtues of the U.S. policy process, there is considerable agreement that power is indeed fragmented and that most regulated groups have a great deal of influence through the multitude of access opportunities that exist. The effect of a more vigorous legislative role on this situation is much less clear. We now turn to this latter issue.

It is perhaps a reflection of the strength of traditional political science concerns with institutional interaction that a structural change is often advocated as a way to reverse the substantive effects of subsystem politics. If mechanisms establishing a legislative role in implementation can be seen as a reclamation of the delegated authority that created subsystem politics in the first place, then it is logical to assume that the successful utilization of these mechanisms will reverse these trends, leading to more aggressive regulation. Expanded legislative authority over implementation would place real checks on unbridled administrative discretion, making it more likely that agencies would regulate in the public interest. Since these arguments are easily misinterpreted or oversimplified, it will be necessary to consider them in some detail.

More directly than anyone else, Lowi places much of the blame for the rise of "interest group liberalism" on congressional delegation of legislative authority. Wide-ranging delegation has occurred, according to Lowi, primarily because of the existence of a congenial public philosophy that accepts the need for it uncritically. The rise of delegation and the corresponding "decline of law" are often attributed to the increasing technological complexity of modern policy, but Lowi finds this rationalization unconvincing. Delegation did not simply expand as policy problems became more technologically complex. In fact, some of the areas in which considerable "legal integrity" still exists are notable for their complexity (he mentions social security law and drug-control law).[20]

Thus, there is no direct relationship between technological complexity and the extent of delegation.

Instead, the fragmentation of public authority is caused by political influences and buttressed by mainstream political and legal thinking. Lowi explains that modern behavioral political science supports the idea of delegated power because it facilitates scientific study of political behavior. If virtually all policy issues were effectively resolved through decisions made at the center of government, there would be few instances of political confrontation, bargaining, or maneuvering elsewhere: "A good law eliminates the political process at certain points." A political system with little delegation of power would be "too formal for modern political science."[21] The theories and prescriptions of modern political science have thus helped to legitimize delegation.

The legal embrace of delegation has been more direct, and probably more influential, than that of mainstream political science. Kenneth C. Davis, one of the most widely recognized scholars in the field of administrative law, fully accepts the idea of delegated legislative power. In fact, he spends nearly an entire chapter of one of his many textbooks arguing against those who would support a more restricted view of delegation. Davis contends that "a modern regulatory agency would probably be an impossibility if power could not be delegated with vague standards."[22] The scope and complexity of modern government makes it necessary for administrators to decide many major substantive questions that cannot be resolved through legislation.[23]

This view of delegation was at odds with a great deal of legal thinking during the New Deal era, as discussed in Chapter 1, and this may be the reason that Davis takes such pains to develop a legal foundation for delegation. Many felt that the combination of legislative, judicial, and executive authority in the hands of appointed administrators would mean the end of freedom for everyone whose activities were within the jurisdiction of an agency. However, Davis argued against this conclusion persuasively along lines that have since become mainstream legal thinking and the basis for several important court decisions. It is impossible to stop or reduce delegation; hence our best defense against arbitrary, unfair administrative actions is, for Davis, the establishment of procedural safeguards and systematic judicial review. In other words, delegate authority to those with the expertise, flexibility, and time to make detailed policy decisions, and rely on legal reforms and judicial review to maintain fairness, accountability, and regularity.[24]

The whole body of administrative law actually grew up around the necessity for these procedural safeguards in the activities of administrative agencies, complete with an establishment of law firms and legal scholars devoted to it. Some have argued that the easy acceptance of delegation by the legal community was a result of the expansion in employment opportunities for lawyers created by the elaboration of administrative procedures.[25] More lawyers have jobs in government and in regulated organizations as a direct consequence of the delegation of power to administrative agencies and the establishment of complicated procedural reforms. However, Davis's idea of procedural safeguards was also persuasive on its own merits. The procedural requirements he advocated were essentially similar to those pertaining to judicial decision-making: on-the-record hearings, rules of evidence, rights to cross-examination and attorney, right to appeal, and so forth. Davis effectively linked the accommodation of delegation to widely accepted legal concepts. Since it appeared that stopping delegation was impossible anyway, the new approach became almost universally accepted.[26]

When the legal acceptance of delegation is fully appreciated, it is easy to understand how an analyst like Lowi attributes the fragmentation of political authority to something as amorphous as a "public philosophy." Moreover, it logically follows that if the cause of "interest group liberalism" is a set of misguided and unfortunate political or legal ideas (Lowi was particularly disturbed by Davis's writing, for example), then the problems can be corrected by changing the structural features attributable to those ideas. In other words, there is nothing wrong with legislators and administrators, and a simple reversal of the trend toward delegation will cure the abuses and inequities resulting from interest-group liberalism.

The reversal may be accomplished, according to this position, without altering legislative motivations. If new mechanisms are established that involve the legislature in administrative decision-making, abuses arising from open-ended delegations of authority will be corrected. Administrators will no longer find themselves adrift from the centers of public responsibility. The legislature will be able to monitor the evolution of public policy, carefully outlining the parameters of the decisions still left to administrative discretion. The policy effect of a greater legislative role would be (in most cases) more effective planning and more aggressive regulatory policy, since the forces it would be correcting would be those that previously moved administrative decisions disproportionately in the direction of sluggish, ineffective regulation.

Lowi specifically mentions two reforms designed to achieve such a reassertion of the rule of law. "Codification" of the policy process would consist of an "effort to systematize, digest, and simplify all of the provisions of law relating to a particular subject."[27] Codification, in this sense, would not always require that enabling legislation address all the questions that inevitably arise as policy is implemented (although Lowi urges Congress to do so as much as possible), but it would require that all administrative and judicial decisions subsequent to initial legislation be incorporated into a coherent body of law. He suggests that legislative committees be empowered to monitor relevant administrative and judicial actions that define public policies, and that they be given authority to reverse decisions that are inconsistent with original legislative intent. Codification would thus place an effective check on special interest influence in agency decision-making. Planning would be more effective, since policy would be predictable and monitored by a central authority.

Sunset laws would have similar effects because the requirement for periodic legislative evaluation and reauthorization of agencies and programs establishes an institutional means of control. They consequently help to correct a basic problem of interest-group liberalism: "the absence of rule of law and the absence of real legislative power to impose it."[28] Like other supporters of sunset, Lowi does not contend that many agencies will actually meet their demise after the laws are in place. The key to reform is its requirement of meaningful legislative evaluation. Pressures arising from the evaluations (and their anticipation by administrators) will force agencies to become more open in their decision-making process, reducing somewhat the influence of regulated and client groups.

The same logic can be applied to other mechanisms of legislative control, particularly committee review of administrative rule-making. This mechanism is often touted, in fact, as a direct antidote for excessive delegation. Harold Bruff and Ernest Gellhorn contend that the current interest in legislature review of rules is a modern-day replacement for the long discredited nondelegation doctrine.[29] Thus, the major form of formal legislative participation in implementation is perhaps the most explicit embodiment of Lowi's hopes for a legislative reassertion.

Although not as elegant as Lowi's argument, there are other lines of reasoning that support the idea that a stronger legislative role would lead to more aggressive regulation. Some have argued that the establishment of a new committee with special administrative review powers would create a "poor man's court" in which individual citizens could obtain redress for grievances against agencies controlled by wealthy organized interests. If we assume that many agencies have been captured by the groups they regulate, the creation of such an alternative access opportunity could provide a means to influence policy in a direction more consistent with the public interest. Proponents of this idea might argue, for example, that a concerned consumer could bring a complaint against the Food and Drug Administration (FDA) before the legislative committee, resulting in a reversal of the agency's allegedly permissive policy of label regulation.

Some supporters of the public advocate movement make similar arguments. Proponents of more aggressive regulation, such as the Sierra Club, Common Cause, and others, often feel that informal channels of communication and influence between regulators and the regulated effectively exclude them from real participation in policy-making. Traditional legislative oversight processes, which normally work through substantive committees, are not thought to correct the imbalances because these committees are themselves part of the subsystems that engender the sluggish regulation. However, the new mechanisms establishing a legislative role in implementation are frequently structurally independent of the subsystem linkages. Joint committees with jurisdiction over all administrative regulations, for example, could theoretically act to uphold broader public interests where they have been denied through subsystem politics, because the general jurisdiction of these committees would make it difficult for the dysfunctional subsystem linkages to develop. Legislative participation would thus tend to make regulation more aggressive and public oriented.

Testimony in recent hearings before the House Judiciary Committee regarding a bill to establish congressional review of administrative rules provides empirical support for this position. Representative John Breckinridge of Kentucky mentioned several instances in which agency decisions were contradictory to legislative intent. Most notably, he asserted that the FDA had established 284 food categories that are exempt from full compliance with the Food, Drug, and Cosmetic Act, despite the act's clear labeling requirements. Moreover, the FDA allegedly

> allows spices, colorings, flavorings, and vegetable oils to be listed simply in general terms rather than by specific names. Products which are exempted by FDA regulations from full compliance with the Act or which provide only a general list of ingredients do not give consumers the type of information that Congress intended them to have.[30]

The noncompliance is apparently quite widespread, according to a General Accounting Office (GAO) report cited by Breckinridge.

Similarly, the Small Business Administration (SBA) allegedly acted contrary to legislative intent in its actions following an earthquake in Alaska in 1964. The SBA granted low-interest loans to persons able to obtain conventional financing and provided disaster loans for the purpose of enlarging property, despite the fact that both practices are contrary to legislative intent.[31]

Breckinridge's thinking on these points is precisely in line with Lowi's argument. A stronger legislative role in the implementation decisions of agencies would, according to the congressman, prevent this kind of administrative action in direct contravention of public law. In the two cases mentioned here, the errant administrative decisions were probably influenced by the kind of clientele or interest group pressures that Lowi finds so damaging. Improved legislative monitoring of administrative rule-making would counter this kind of influence if, as Lowi and others argue, the legislators involved are interested in preserving legislative objectives.

CONCLUSION

The idea that a stronger legislative presence in agency decision-making would lead to more aggressive regulation is based on important assumptions regarding the political context of regulation and the character of legislative influence. In its simplest forms, the argument assumes that regulatory agencies are responsive to the inputs they receive, and that the most effective inputs, for several reasons, are from the groups they regulate. The absence of central or party control of legislative power leads to the development of subsystems, which make policy decisions that operate independently and with little regard for the public interest.

Optimistic analysts accepting this view of the policy process quite logically advocate structural reforms that are designed to counteract subsystem linkages. New mechanisms for legislative participation in implementation may be interpreted as effective ways to reestablish central control at the expense of irresponsible subsystem politics. Expanded legislative participation would therefore lead to more aggressive regulation in those cases in which regulatory policy has been moderated at the behest of regulated and client groups.

It should be noted that this position is in some ways inconsistent with the essential thesis of the first chapter. If legislative participation in implementation is a reaction to changes in patterns of political influence and not an effort to reassert legislative intent, much of the theorizing in this chapter is based on faulty assumptions. The idea that legislative participation facilitates regulatory aggressiveness is, particularly for Lowi, compelling because of a belief that legislators will attempt to maintain administrative adherence to legislative intent if given adequate powers to do so. If we assume that legislators are not motivated primarily by such a desire, the argument loses much of its force.

However, accepting the thesis of Chapter 1 does not lead unavoidably to the conclusion that legislative participation cannot facilitate regulatory aggressiveness. Even if legislators are not motivated in the ways Lowi implies, it is possible that the new forms of legislative influence facilitate regulatory aggressiveness because they are structurally independent of the policy subsystems. The balance of political forces acting on joint rule review committees, for example, may be significantly different from the balance of forces in the subsystems; thus decisions contrary to the narrow subsystem interests may be imposed by legislative control mechanisms despite the absence of an explicit motivation to monitor legislative intent. The FDA episode discussed above could be consistent with this interpretation.

In short, the arguments presented here do not depend entirely on unrealistic expectations regarding legislative motivations, but are based on generally cogent arguments that can be supported by actual administrative experience. The broad delegation of public authority to administrators has certainly made a great deal of private interest influence possible, and it is arguable that a return of a measure of this discretion to central legislative control could effectively counter it. However, there are persuasive arguments in the opposite direction, based primarily on a rejection of the second part of the proposition articulated in this chapter. If the new mechanisms of legislative participation do not work to monitor compliance with legislative intent, and if there are reasons to assume that the balance of political influences acting on these mechanisms is disproportionately opposed to aggressive regulation, a completely different set of outcomes is possible.

NOTES

1. Woodrow Wilson, Congressional Government (New York: Meridian Books, 1956; originally published 1885), p. 195.

2. Seymour Scher, "Conditions for Legislative Control," Journal of Politics, Vol. 25 (August 1963), p. 526.

3. J. S. Mill, Representative Government, quoted in Cornelius P. Cotter, "Legislative Oversight," in Congress: The First Branch, Alfred de Grazia, ed. (Washington, D.C.: American Enterprise Institute, 1966), p. 25.

4. Edgar Crane, Jr., Legislative Review of Government Programs: Tools for Accountability (New York: Praeger, 1977), p. 3. Crane's quote is an attributed paraphrase of Max Weber.

5. Joseph P. Harris, Congressional Control of Administration (Washington, D.C.: Brookings, 1964), p. 1.

6. Jacob Javits, quoted in John H. Sheridan, "Can Congress Control the Regulators?" Industry Week, Vol. 188 (March 29, 1976), p. 22.

7. Ernest S. Griffith, The Impasse of Democracy, quoted in Emmette S. Redford, Democracy in the Administrative State (New York: Oxford University Press, 1969), p. 96.

8. See J. Leiper Freeman, *The Political Process: Executive Bureau--Legislative Committee Relations* (New York: Random House, 1955); and, for a discussion directly pertaining to oversight, Lawrence C. Dodd and Richard L. Schott, *Congress and the Administrative State* (New York: Wiley, 1979), pp. 170-184.

9. Freeman, p. 22.

10. Norton E. Long, "Power and Administration," in *Bureaucratic Power in National Politics*, 3d ed., Francis E. Rourke, ed. (Boston: Little, Brown, 1978), p. 9.

11. Redford, *Democracy in the Administrative State*, ch. 8.

12. Harvey Lieber, "Public Administration and Environmental Quality," *Public Administration Review*, Vol. 30 (May-June 1970), pp. 277-286.

13. Aaron Wildavsky, *The Politics of the Budgetary Process*, 3d ed. (Boston: Little, Brown, 1979), pp. 192-193.

14. Theodore Lowi, *The End of Liberalism*, 2d ed. (New York: Norton, 1979), ch. 4.

15. Marver Bernstein, *Regulating Business by Independent Commission* (Princeton: Princeton University Press, 1955).

16. Quoted in Milton Friedman and Rose Friedman, *Free to Choose* (New York: Harcourt Brace Jovanovich, 1980), p. 167.

17. Ibid.

18. The second edition of *The End of Liberalism* includes a "sketch of a constitution" of the "Second Republic" of the United States intended to show how the government actually operates. Among other provisions, Lowi's bleak description of contemporary political institutions includes the following statement: "Congress must take care never to draft a careful and precise statute because this would interfere with the judgment of the president and his professional and full-time administrators." Lowi, p. xii.

19. Ibid., pp. 116-119.

20. Ibid., pp. 158, 204.

21. Ibid., p. 93.

22. Kenneth C. Davis, *Administrative Law and Government*, 2d ed. (St. Paul: West, 1975), p. 43.

23. Ibid. Also, for an excellent legal history of the concept of delegation, see Glen Robinson, Ernest Gellhorn, and Harold Bruff, *The Administrative Process*, 2d ed. (St. Paul: West, 1980), ch. 2.

24. This idea is developed, with some reliance on Davis's writing, in an important judicial decision. See Fook Hong Mak v. Immigration and Naturalization Service, 435 F.2d 728 (1970).

25. This possibility was suggested by an early opponent of the Federal Administrative Procedure Act of 1946. See Frederick F. Blachly, "Critique of the Federal Administrative Procedure Act," in The Federal Administrative Procedure Act and the Administrative Agencies, George Warren, ed. (New York: New York University School of Law, 1947), pp. 30-34.

26. As Davis flatly asserts, judicial opinions holding that legislative power cannot lawfully be delegated are "unrealistic verbiage" that "should not now be taken seriously." Davis, p. 39.

27. Lowi, pp. 305-309.

28. Ibid., p. 307.

29. Harold H. Bruff and Ernest Gellhorn, "Congressional Control of Administrative Regulation: A Study of Legislative Vetoes," Harvard Law Review, Vol. 90 (May 1977), p. 1373.

30. Subcommittee on Administrative Law and Governmental Relations of the House Judiciary Committee, U.S. Congress, Hearings: Congressional Review of Administrative Rule-Making (Washington, D.C.: U.S. Government Printing Office, 1975), p. 206.

31. Ibid.

3

LEGISLATIVE PARTICIPATION AS AN INHIBITOR OF REGULATORY AGGRESSIVENESS

Many years ago, a federal official proposed the following as his idea of a perfect enabling statute for the Radio Commission:

> Section 1: That a licensing authority is hereby created and established to be known as the Radio Czar of America.
> Section 2: The Radio Czar created by Section 1 shall do the best he can.
> Section 3: For the purpose of this Act the U.S. is divided into two zones, as follows:
>
> > The first zone shall embrace the area comprised within a circle having a radius of one block to be drawn around the office of the Radio Czar; the second zone shall comprise the rest of the United States, its territories, and possessions.
>
> Section 4: It is hereby expressly forbidden that any Senator, Congressman, politician, president of a women's club, or broadcaster shall set foot within the first zone, under penalty of capital punishment.[1]

Administrators have frequently complained about intrusions from external sources. They are, it seems, constantly frustrated by the queries, requests, and demands that reduce administrative efficiency and confuse otherwise neat lines of authority. Although private groups have always been an important source of such influences, the legislature is becoming one of the most troublesome intruders, according to many bureaucrats. If the legislature would simply establish policy objectives and provide funding, the administrator's job would be much more manageable.

The traditional administrative aversion to legislative participation is based on a lofty view of administrative expertise and motives, reinforced by mainstream public administration theorizing. Legislative involvement in agency decision-making simply has no place in Weber's classical bureaucratic organization. Consequently, nearly a century of administrative study has systematically excluded consideration of legislative influence in the everyday workings of public agencies.[2] It should not be surprising that the emergence of new mechanisms allowing legislators to participate in administrative decisions is viewed by bureaucrats with frustration and irritation. Thirty-five of 45 federal administrators indicated their opinion of the trend toward state legislative appropriation of federal funds to state agencies by asserting that they would "ignore" any actions taken by the state legislators.[3] Similar responses are common when other new mechanisms of legislative control are proposed or enacted.[4]

These expressions of impatience with legislative involvement are partly a function of the fact that most administrators have become socialized to their profession during a period of little legislative participation in their affairs. While constituent service has always been an important activity for legislators, its effect on administrative policy decisions has generally been minimal.[5] The primary instrument of legislative influence on the substance of agency policy has been control of the annual budget. Everyday administrative operations, including nearly all administrative rule-making and other formal actions, have traditionally taken place with little legislative involvement.

As discussed in Chapter 1, new approaches to legislative involvement have changed the situation fundamentally. State legislatures and Congress have adopted powers that extend the scope of their control well beyond the establishment of policy objectives and funding levels. Keefe and Ogul concluded that through the use of the legislative veto and similar devices

> Congress projects itself or one of its committees into the administrative decision-making process. Instead of exercising oversight by setting conditions for action in legislation, by checking on past executive activity, or by investigating conduct, Congress assumes a direct role in the process.[6]

A similar conclusion applies to the use of these devices in the states. When we realize that the new forms of legislative participation actually displace a meaningful share of agency discretion, administrative resistance is easily understood, even if not wholly justifiable.

The idea that the policy effect of this new legislative involvement is to inhibit regulatory aggressiveness is based on a different view of legislative behavior than that expressed by the analysts discussed in Chapter 2. Lowi and others suggest that a stronger legislative presence can potentially act as a centralizing force, reasserting the intent of law where overbroad delegation of authority has led to a disintegration of public purpose. The keystone of the counterargument is that, instead of strengthening the rule of law in administrative decision-making, the new mechanisms of legislative participation themselves create additional sources of fragmentation.

This second view thus discounts the importance of the distinctive structural features of the new legislative control mechanisms that are supposed to make them counteract subsystem linkages. It similarly rejects any contention that legislators are motivated by a desire to safeguard legislative intent when using their new powers. Finally, and most important, this position argues that there are reasons to believe that the access opportunities created by legislative participation are, in practice, disproportionately useful to regulated and client groups.

LEGISLATIVE PROCESSES AND INTEREST GROUP INFLUENCE

The idea that regulated interests will benefit disproportionately from legislative participation is based on several basic assumptions about the nature of political influence in the implementation process. First, according to some analysts, the fact that the formal procedures of legislative committees are not governed by the legal requirements governing agency actions makes it unlikely that legislative participation will facilitate regulatory aggressiveness. Agency rule-making procedures have become increasingly elaborate during the last 30 years, requiring extensive notice periods, publication of proposed rules and notices of hearings, and on-the-record decisions. Rule-making decisions can often be appealed in court to determine whether the rules are consistent with applicable statutes and constitutional provisions.[7] These procedural requirements, which do not apply to legislative committee activities, make administrative hearings truly open to public participation from all affected parties. The less-formalized legislative committee hearings can be held almost privately at the behest of special interests opposing aggressive regulatory decisions made in agency hearings.

Consequently, the administrative rule-making process, termed "one of the greatest inventions of modern government" by one noted scholar, may be compromised by the availability of new forms of legislative participation in implementation.[8] The basic purpose of rule-making reforms is the achievement of access for all participants, a value formally achieved through rigid hearing requirements. Bruff and Gellhorn, in their pioneering study of legislative vetoes on the federal level, concluded that a committee review process makes this public participation before agencies less meaningful:

> There were indications that the veto machinery may have created opportunities for circumvention of public participation. In certain subtle ways, the presence of Congressional review allowed the influence of special interest groups in Congress to affect the substance of rules outside the comment process.[9]

The fact that administrative decisions can be changed through subsequent legislative committee review decisions reduces the importance of any public comments, suggestions, and information provided in the agency hearing.

Bruff and Gellhorn imply that the policy effect of this change in the rule-making process will be an increase in the frequency of decisions favorable to regulated interests at the expense of the general public. Their argument makes an important assumption about the interest group context of regulation--an assumption that can easily be challenged. Simply put, they feel that regulated interests are more capable of using the relatively unreformed legislative hearings to their advantage than are proregulatory forces or the general public. Hence, legislative involvement in agency decision-making will ultimately lead to more moderate regulatory policy.

There are reasons to support this view regardless of one's conclusions about the desirability of aggressive regulation and the representativeness of "public advocate" organizations. The most persuasive argument has to do with the different strategies followed by pro- and antiregulatory forces. The reformist zeal of many public advocate groups leads them to focus their efforts on the early stages of policy formulation. Consequently, they are likely to participate in the formal, well-publicized rule-making hearings, since these hearings are generally the occasions for initial announcement and definition of agency policy.[10] Although regulated groups are also highly concerned about initial policy-formulation decisions, their interests are often quite specific and sometimes technical in nature. They naturally find the later legislative committee hearing more congenial. It provides an opportunity to discuss a particular aspect of a regulatory decision without becoming involved in arguments over the rationale for the whole policy.

Moreover, the fact that some interests have greater financial and legal resources than others suggests that legislative participation in implementation will reduce the overall representativeness of the policy process. Since "not all interested parties have the resources both to participate in the public comment proceedings and to lobby the committees effectively in the review process," the establishment of the committee veto of agency decisions enlarges the gap between the powerful and less powerful interests.[11] Although the growth of public advocate groups during the last few years has changed things considerably, many still believe that regulated and client groups are better equipped to participate in complex governmental proceedings than the proregulatory forces. Mechanisms for legislative involvement in implementation constitute an additional step in the policy process, a change detrimental to interests whose resources are strained by lobbying for enabling legislation and by participation in initial agency hearings. The ultimate effect of this imbalance in resources is to increase the importance of financial capacity in determining the strength of political influence.

Moreover, legislative participation may also be especially helpful to regulated groups because of changes in their own linkages with government agencies. The first major effort at government regulation of business was the establishment of the regulatory commissions, beginning with the ICC in 1887. Through the 1940s, regulated groups were normally subject to regulation by only one bureau, the commission established especially to regulate their activities. It is not difficult to stay aware of regulatory decisions affecting one's activities when a single agency is the source of all or nearly all of them. It is also relatively easy to influence those decisions.

Government regulation during the last two decades has not only increased in scope; its complexity has also grown substantially. Nearly all business enterprises must now deal with regulatory decisions made by environmental protection agencies, occupational safety agencies, equal opportunity agencies, and others, often including agencies on both the state and federal levels in each category.[12] Effective political participation in opposition to aggressive regulation thus requires that regulated interests spread their political energies quite widely. Regulated interests may support the idea of committee review of agency decisions because it would allow them to concentrate their opposition to aggressive regulation at a single point.[13]

Legislative participation in implementation may thus play a unique role in relation to subsystem politics. Regulated groups that have been successful in their attempts to influence the agency of most importance to them (that is, their subsystem partners) do not advocate the establishment of new legislative controls. Policy is adequately under their influence through the subsystem linkages. However, when a regulated group is faced with regulation by other forces, it must turn elsewhere for relief. A new legislative committee with special authority over administrative decisions would be a particularly appropriate access opportunity for this type of complaint. If correct, this notion would help to explain why the expansion of legislative participation in implementation is a relatively recent phenomenon. Legislative participation is not a response to regulation itself, which, after all, has been extensive for nearly 100 years, but is instead a reaction to regulation from agencies outside traditional subsystem linkages (or from agencies no longer working within established subsystem perspectives). The recent establishment of new regulatory agencies with overlapping functional jurisdictions ensures that an increasing proportion of regulatory activity will be outside the normal subsystem relationships. Mechanisms enabling a small segment of the legislature to change regulatory decisions thus become increasingly valuable to the regulated as their ability to control regulatory policy is reduced.

A final reason for asserting that a stronger legislative role in implementation works, on balance, to the benefit of the regulated is based on an understanding of the timing of legislative actions in implementation. Consider two situations: Case A--an aggressive legislative mandate is enacted by the legislature and implemented by a regulatory agency, and Case B--no legislative mandate is enacted. In our simple zero-sum model of the regulatory process, the regulated interests would be aroused to take action in Case A while Case B would arouse disgruntled public advocates. Having failed to block passage of the enabling legislation or the implementing regulations, regulated groups would turn to the reviewing committee for relief in the scenario of Case A. If they are able to find a few sympathetic committee members (who themselves may have opposed the original legislative decision), the committee action will lead to a moderation of original regulatory policy.

Public advocates can theoretically follow a parallel course in Case B. However, if no regulatory legislation has been passed, the reviewing committee will not have jurisdiction to respond to their complaints, since there is no statute for which regulations will have been promulgated. Thus, situations in which public advocates are disappointed will simply result in more vigorous lobbying by them for enabling legislation (or for administrative action under existing statutory authority). If the legislative mechanisms are seen as working to "put out fires," it is probable that their actions will disproportionately be designed to moderate regulation, since the inputs they are most likely to receive will consist of reactions to regulations already promulgated and not those yet to be written.[14]

In short, the "slippage" between original legislative enactments and later legislative participation in implementation, if it occurs, is more likely to favor regulated interests than proregulatory forces or the general public. The fact that committee decisions can be rescinded by actions of the entire legislature diminishes this possibility, but it does not eliminate its importance. Even if an agency can expect to be vindicated by later assembly action, the committee's reviewing authority can be an important source of delay, and thus, a source of influence. The situation enables legislative participants to exercise a measure of independent control over the implementing agency despite the fact that its decisions may not be final in a legal sense.

If these lines of reasoning are valid, the advent of legislative participation in implementation is a persuasive confirmation of Edelman's arguments concerning symbolic politics. He contends that regulatory programs are often enacted to satisfy abstract demands for action, and that implementation typically falls short of initial expectations. A policy is thus able to succeed on a symbolic level while failing to achieve its ostensible purpose. If the new mechanisms of legislative involvement provide an access opportunity more useful to regulated groups than to proregulatory forces or the general public, then the institutional structure may itself contribute to the gap between the symbolic and the real in policy implementation. Legislative involvement through later and less visible committee proceedings may work to take the teeth out of programs that previously secured legislative support.[15]

Despite these arguments, the actual policy impact of legislative participation remains an empirical question. Research discussed in later chapters will address the issue directly, but it is appropriate at this point to acknowledge that the prior expectations of several different organizations influential in the policy process are largely in accordance with the idea that a stronger legislative role will moderate regulatory aggressiveness.

In Chapter 2 we referred to a report of hearings before a subcommittee of the House Judiciary Committee in which a member of Congress brought forth examples of agency regulations that were notably less aggressive than would be expected on the basis of expressed legislative intent.[16] There are reasons to believe that this kind of deviation is exceptional. A number of private groups and government administrative personnel also testified at those hearings, and all but two of the presentations were either decidedly for or decidedly against the idea of legislative committee review of agency rules. The breakdown of support and opposition is shown in Table 3.1.

Table 3.1 Support and Opposition from Private Groups and Agency Officials for Committee Rule Review, as Expressed in House Judiciary Hearings

Supporters	Opponents
Members of House of Delegates, American Medical Association	Deputy Assistant Secretary, Occupational Health and Safety Administration
American Hospital Association	Assistant Secretary, Health, Education, and Welfare
Washington Counsel, National Federation of Independent Business	General Counsel, Federal Trade Commission
American Sub-Contractors Association	Legal Counsel, Department of Justice
American Dental Association	General Counsel, Environmental Protection Agency
American Osteopathic Hospital Association	American Nurses Association
Southeastern Poultry and Egg Association	
Board of Supervisors, Los Angeles County	
Federation of American Hospitals	

Source: Statements of support and opposition by these persons were made in October and November 1975, as reported in: Subcommittee on Administrative Law and Governmental Relations of the House Judiciary Committee, Hearings: Congressional Review of Administrative Rule-Making (Washington, D.C.: U.S. Government Printing Office, 1975), pp. 285-514.

If this is any indication, it is clear that opponents of aggressive regulation expect that legislative review will help them to moderate agency decisions. The most obvious point in the table is the near unanimity with which the business and professional groups supported the mechanism and the complete unanimity with which agency officials opposed it. In light of the previous discussions, it is also interesting to note some of the reasons given for support and opposition. The bulk of the support for committee review authority came from various groups connected with health care delivery. Many of their presentations included heated complaints, not only about the extent of regulation, but also about the wide variety of agencies that regulate their activities. Several spokespersons complained that the regulatory situation is chaotic, uncoordinated, and unpredictable. A special committee empowered to suspend agency regulations is, to them, an attractive antidote for these problems.

The American Nurses Association was the only private group that opposed the mechanism, but their reasoning suggests why their position may be exceptional. Like the other health care organizations, the nurses complained that "executive implementation of the law" is occasionally inconsistent with "original Congressional intentions," but they did not feel that committee review was an appropriate solution. Instead, they advocated improved conditions for public participation. Their suggestions indicate that their association may have had more success in dealing with regulators than the hospitals and doctors' organizations:

> We see a need for the retention of some latitude in the exercise of administrative judgment by the various agencies of the executive branch of the government, coupled with the increased participation of the <u>appropriate publics</u> in the rule-making process wherever possible.[17]

Legislative involvement in agency decision-making is opposed by the nurses apparently because they still feel confident that they can make the subsystem linkages serve their interests.

Although the perspective of this Nurses Association is important, it is striking that virtually all other private groups subject to extensive government regulation have supported the idea of legislative committee involvement in agency decision-making. The widespread assumption is that committee review is a way to restrain overzealous administrators who exceed their statutory authority or who simply restrict private activity excessively. Typical supporters of the mechanism assert that effective legislative review would have corrected, for example, a Labor Department decision requiring contractors to pay prevailing rates for commercial construction where the applicable statute intended that they be required to pay the lower rates for residential construction.[18] Many other examples are available along the same lines.[19] Clearly, the predominant assumption of regulated interests and those representing them is that legislative participation will help to get agencies off their backs.

CONCLUSION

The fundamental argument of this chapter begins with a critical assumption regarding legislative behavior. The absence of systematic, responsible, coordinated oversight activities is not seen as a function of insufficient legislative authority. Instead, the inherently fragmented nature of legislative power is allegedly at fault. Legislative committees normally operate with a degree of independence, enabling each to exert influence in directions not always representative of legislative majorities or party platforms. The introduction of special committee powers over agency decisions in such a setting is expected to create serious difficulties, particularly for the aggressive implementation of regulatory policy.

Specifically, legislative participation in implementation is expected to inhibit regulatory aggressiveness because: committee hearings are less representative than administrative hearings; regulated interests are more likely than public advocates to have the resources necessary to make effective use of the additional participative opportunity created by the new legislative presence; the contrasting strategies of public advocates and regulated interests make legislative participation a more appropriate access opportunity for the latter; regulated interests are more attracted to legislative participation than are public advocates because regulated groups must deal with more agencies than public advocates; and the formal jurisdiction of legislative control mechanisms suggests that they will be used more often to respond to complaints about onerous proposed regulations than to respond to the absence of aggressive regulation.

NOTES

1. "The Standard of Public Interest, Convenience, or Necessity as Used in Radio Act of 1927," Air Law Review, Vol. 1 (1930), p. 259, as quoted in Cornelius P. Cotter, "Legislative Oversight," in Congress: The First Branch, ed. Alfred de Grazia (Washington, D.C.: American Enterprise Institute, 1966), pp. 35-36.

2. John A. Worthley, Public Administration and Legislatures (Chicago: Nelson-Hall, 1976), chs. 1-3.

3. Patricia K. Freeman and E. Fletcher McClellan, The Consequences of Increased Legislative Oversight of Federal Funds: The Case of Tennessee (Knoxville, Tenn.: Bureau of Public Administration, 1981), p. 2.

4. Joseph Harris surveys many of these complaints in Congressional Control of Administration (Washington, D.C.: Brookings, 1964).

5. However, John R. Johannes suggests that although constituent service activities usually do not change the substance or direction of policy, they can stimulate "self-correcting action." See "Casework as a Technique of U.S. Congressional Oversight," Legislative Studies Quarterly, Vol. 4 (August 1979), pp. 325-352.

6. William J. Keefe and Morris S. Ogul, The American Legislative Process, 4th ed. (Englewood Cliffs, N.J.: Prentice-Hall, 1977), p. 391.

7. Harold H. Bruff and Ernest Gellhorn, "Congressional Control of Administrative Regulation: A Case Study of Legislative Vetoes," Harvard Law Review, Vol. 90 (May 1977), p. 1413.

8. Kenneth C. Davis, Administrative Law and Government, 2d ed. (St. Paul: West, 1975), p. 121.

9. Bruff and Gellhorn, p. 1413.

10. In the context of environmental policy, for example, it has been argued that the amount of lead time and the extent of advertisement of rule-making hearings have a significant effect on public advocate effectiveness. See Lynton Caldwell, Lynton Hayes, and Isabel MacWhirter, Citizens and the Environment (Bloomington: Indiana University Press, 1976), pp. xxiii-xxv.

11. Bruff and Gellhorn, p. 1414.

12. Alan Stone, Regulation and Its Alternatives (Washington, D.C.: Congressional Quarterly Press, 1982), p. 32.

13. This idea was suggested by an aide to Representative Elliot Levitas (D.-Ga.) in a telephone interview in August 1977. Levitas's staff, which had been working on a rule review bill for some time, noted that interests that were governed by a single agency were less supportive of new oversight controls.

14. This fact alone doubtlessly accounts for the popular support for rule review expressed by opponents of restrictive regulatory policy. See John H. Sheridan, "Can Congress Control the Regulators?" Industry Week, Vol. 188 (March 29, 1976), pp. 20-27.

15. Murray Edelman, The Symbolic Uses of Politics (Champaign-Urbana: University of Illinois Press, 1964), ch. 2.

16. Subcommittee on Administrative Law and Governmental Relations of the House Judiciary Committee, U.S. Congress, Hearings: Congressional Review of Administrative Rule-Making (Washington, D.C.: U.S. Government Printing Office, 1975).

17. Ibid., p. 250, emphasis added.

18. Ibid., p. 206.

19. See Sheridan, pp. 24-27.

4

LEGISLATURES AND IMPLEMENTATION: A QUESTION OF STRUCTURE AND INFLUENCE

The positions discussed in the two preceding chapters are based on very different perspectives regarding legislatures, administrators, and public policies. Conflicts regarding the values of representativeness and efficiency are also apparent when the logic underlying the positions is critically examined. However, the debate is not entirely a question of which values should be pursued at the expense of others; it also contains issues that are subject to empirical verification. In this chapter we will consider the essential differences among these positions and two subsidiary positions so that the implications of resolving any questions amenable to scientific research can be fully appreciated.

The predictions of the ideas presented in Chapters 2 and 3 are contradictory on the question of the effect of legislative participation on regulatory aggressiveness. However, it is important to note that this disagreement does not stem from simple assumptions about the substantive preference of legislators. It would be a mundane problem indeed if the disagreement were a matter of one school of thought holding that legislators are typically conservative on regulatory policy issues while the other held that they are liberal. The reason that the debate over the policy impact of a greater legislative role is a compelling one is that it reflects a fundamental disagreement over the motivations, capacities, and power of legislatures in the implementation process. Determining how expanded legislative involvement affects regulatory aggressiveness may contribute to our understanding of the overall representativeness and effectiveness of our government institutions.

THE GUIDING ASSUMPTIONS

An essential feature of the first position--a stronger legislative role in implementation facilitates aggressiveness--is the assumption that the legal or institutional position of legislators and administrators is important in determining their behavior. Legislators are expected to be highly involved in their function of law-making. They are consequently oriented toward defending legislative decisions in cases of explicit opposition from executive, administrative, or judicial institutions. Legislation is their primary instrument of power and it is argued that they are interested in maintaining the integrity of legislative mandates. Consequently, the creation of new powers over administrative decisions will be utilized primarily for the purpose of enforcing legislative intent.

Administrators also are expected to develop an operating perspective that is derived from the nature of their activities. The detailed, technical nature of many regulatory decisions requires that administrators work closely with the groups they regulate, even joining the same professional associations in some cases. Their work leads to an identification of purpose that is frequently quite specialized. Administrators in agriculture departments think of themselves as working for the improvement of farming and the lives of farmers, not only because they may be "captured" by special interests, but because they are naturally oriented to these ends by their tasks. The same point can be made about administrators who pursue equal opportunity, regulation of nuclear power, environmental protection, and other policy objectives.[1]

The specificity of administrative objectives, coupled with the inevitable linkages to regulated groups, has unarguably resulted in administrative action in contradiction of legislative intent, as Lowi and others contend. Administrators feel they are aware of the problems and solutions in their field and that the legislature has only vague ideas often distorted by ignorance, political influence, or ideology. The first position implies that this elitist bureaucratic perspective leads to administrative decisions that overrepresent the interests of the regulated whenever agency officials have sufficient discretion.

If the problem is caused by institutional factors, it is reasonable to expect that its cure consists of legal or structural changes. New mechanisms of legislative control would presumably enable legislators to assert the rule of law over administrators. Such a reassertion would have a real political impact because of the different formal positions of legislators and administrators; the mechanisms would help to neutralize agency-interest group linkages that jeopardize legislative intent and reduce regulatory aggressiveness.

The keys to this position are the assumptions that legislators are guided by their legal status as lawmakers, and the new mechanisms of legislative control are structurally independent of subsystem politics. Paradoxically, another view can be supported on the basis of these same assumptions, one that predicts that legislative participation has a policy effect opposite to that predicted by the position discussed in Chapter 2. If the first version can be considered roughly "progressive" (in that it advocates a reduction of private interest influence), this second version is clearly conservative. The major difference between the two versions has to do with the supposed cause of administrative irresponsibility. The Lowi-based argument assumes that administrative irresponsibility stems from agency linkages to those they regulate, but the conservative argument assumes that it is a function of excessive administrative zeal, myopia, and bureaucratic disregard for cost-benefit calculations.[2]

If this second version is correct about the causes of administrative irresponsibility, then the reassertion of public purpose by legislators newly endowed with independent powers over implementation will not shift the substance of policy in the direction that Lowi and other progressive reformers predict. The conservative supporters of a stronger legislative role in implementation predict that reforms will moderate regulatory policy. It is expected that legislators armed with new review powers will act to eliminate wasteful regulations and unwanted restrictions on business designed by unaccountable bureaucrats driven only by their extreme ideologies. Nonetheless, both versions share an essential and fundamental assumption: properly empowered legislators will act to uphold the rule of law where it has been abrogated by irresponsible bureaucrats.

These positions are therefore classified under the term "legal-accountability."

The position discussed in Chapter 3 is wholly different in that it discounts the importance of legal position and asserts that patterns of influence in the regulatory process will determine both legislative and administrative behavior. The impact of any structural manipulations must be evaluated in light of this assumption. Since "legislative intent" is not sufficiently meaningful to shape and direct oversight activities, legislators are expected to respond to the inputs they receive, which, for several reasons discussed previously, are expected to favor regulated interests. The conclusion that an expanded legislative role in implementation will therefore reduce regulatory aggressiveness is identical to the conclusion drawn from the conservative version of the legal-accountability position. The grounds for the conclusion differ, of course, as do the normative evaluations. The conservative supporters of the legal-accountability position see moderated regulatory decisions resulting from a stronger legislative role because legislators will be able to restrain overdriven bureaucratic zealots; supporters of the Chapter 3 position see moderated regulatory decisions as resulting from the increased dominance of policy implementation by regulated interests made possible by the legislative changes.

Little is said about administrative motivations in Chapter 3; the essential feature of that position is its assumption regarding the balance of influences acting on legislators when participating in implementation decisions. However, it is implied that the administrators are in some measure insulated from the immediate pressures that act upon legislators. The most commonly held reasons for such a conclusion have to do with the longer time perspective of appointed officials and their supposed adherence to professional standards.[3] The introduction of legislative participation is thought to frustrate regulatory aggressiveness because it amplifies the influence of the regulated over otherwise public-spirited and professional administrators. This basis for rejecting a stronger legislative role (and the fact that many administrators apparently support such a view) makes it appropriate to classify it as the "planning-administrative" position.

Thus we see that the debate over the policy consequences of a stronger legislative role is intricately related to a larger, long-standing controversy regarding institutional relationships. Both legal-accountability positions are based on a firm belief in constitutional foundations. Legislators and administrators are not simply clear vessels to be filled with whatever influences are most important at the moment; their behavior and perspectives are shaped by their formal institutional status. While a highly persuasive view in some contexts, the ambiguity of the legal-accountability approach is revealed by the contrasting policy expectations that can be drawn from it. The planning-administrative position discounts the importance of legal position, agreeing with the more modern political science perspective that holds that patterns of political responsibility, both formal and informal, determine policy outcomes. However, administrators are somehow immune to the more disintegrative influences, according to this position. New mechanisms of legislative participation in implementation would only subject administrators to the vagaries of political interest, while utterly failing to reassert public purpose.

A final, more balanced perspective completes the main approaches to the problem. This view supports an expanded legislative role in implementation because it assumes that the representativeness of the policy process is obtained not by legislative adherence to the rule of law or by administrative adherence to the rule of law or by administrative adherence to professional standards, but by maximizing the number and type of political access opportunities in the policy process. This general conclusion is widely supported in pluralist writings, but it has been applied specifically to legislative-administrative relations most directly in Aaron Wildavsky's work on the budgetary process.[4] His vehement rejection of administrative and scientific "rationality" in the budgetary process is tied to a corresponding acceptance of legislative influence. Wildavsky argues that the incremental, fragmented nature of legislative power nurtures representation (by allowing all important interests to exert some influence), and its negative impact on administrative coordination and "rationality" can be substantially discounted.[5] True "political rationality" requires that we abandon administrative efforts to achieve objective solutions. A multiplicity of access points holds the greatest potential for a representative and effective policy process, and legislative participation in implementation creates several new access points.[6] The assumptions and values supported by this line of reasoning justify its designation as the "pluralistic-accountability" position.

The two versions of the legal-accountability position, the planning-administrative position, and the pluralistic-accountability position together constitute a comprehensive list of the major perspectives on the issue of legislative participation in implementation. Their differences and similarities are summarized in Table 4.1. The strong political support for the development of new legislative control mechanisms on both the state and national levels is perhaps more clearly understandable when the major perspectives are directly compared; Table 4.1 illustrates that three of the four positions advocate a stronger legislative presence. The normative assumptions are quite different, however, as are the expectations regarding policy consequences. Determining empirically how the new mechanisms actually affect policy will help to resolve some of the major disagreements regarding legislative-administrative relationships in the policy process.

The most direct and important implications of empirical analysis of the policy effects of the new legislative control mechanisms have to do with its impact on subsystem politics. The progressive legal-accountability position holds that a stronger legislative presence exerted through new structures would counteract subsystem linkages; the conservative version at least implies that new legislative controls would augment them, particularly the linkages between regulator and regulated. There is a large body of social and political analysis that criticizes the effects of subsystem politics, blaming it for everything from the military-industrial complex to anticompetitive restrictions on trade. Determining whether a structural legislative change combats or expands subsystem politics would be of considerable practical and theoretical significance.

Moreover, determining whether legislative participation in implementation inhibits or facilitates regulatory aggressiveness will provide a strong indication of the extent to which legislators acting in reviewing committees and/or individually are guided by an effort to police administrative actions in violation of legislative intent. If any structural reforms actually lead legislators to perform such a function, the integrity of legislative intent would be improved, thereby increasing the integration of policy formulation and implementation.[7] These are large issues not to be resolved by a single inquiry, but a careful

Table 4.1 Major Approaches to the Problem

Positions	Evaluation of an Expanded Legislative Role	Representational Potential of Administrators	Representational Potential Legislators	Expected Impact of Expanded Legislative Role
Legal-Accountability				
Progressive	Positive	Low (due to special interest influence)	Supportive of Public Interest	Increased Regulatory Aggressiveness
Conservative	Positive	Low (due to overzealousness, myopia)	Supportive of Public Interest	Decreased Regulatory Aggressiveness
Planning-Administrative	Negative	High (responsive to professional goals and standards)	Responsive to Private Interests	Decreased Regulatory Aggressiveness
Pluralistic-Accountability	Positive	Moderate (responsive to influences gaining access)	Responsive to Representative Array of Interests	No Consistent Effect

investigation of the policy impact of the new legislative controls will have direct bearing on them.

If the highly questionable assumption that legislators acting in implementation simply guard legislative intent is rejected, it is still possible that legislators are influenced by some interests more than others. The comfortable assumptions of the pluralistic-accountability position depend, in part, on the existence of relatively equal access opportunities for identifiable interests. If the politics of implementation operate to make legislative participation more useful to the regulated than others (as suggested in Chapter 3), it will be difficult to be sanguine about the development of increasingly powerful mechanisms for legislative participation. Research establishing how the new mechanisms affect the substance of policy may help to determine the representativeness of the access opportunities they provide.

Finally, such research may reveal something about the nature and extent of public advocate influence in regulatory policy implementation. It is clear that these groups have considerable influence at some points of the policy process, particularly policy formulation and initiation. However, their success with legislators has been less impressive. If legislative review committees work conspicuously for or against the interests of public advocates when participating in implementation, we will have a strong suggestion as to these groups' actual role in influencing legislators through the new access opportunities.

Of course, determining the policy effect of expanded legislative participation will not answer some important questions. If research indicates that a stronger legislative role leads to decreased regulatory aggressiveness, for example, it is not possible to say (on the basis of such a finding) whether previous policy decisions were aggressive because of administrative "professionalism" or because of administrative "myopia." Relatedly, it will not contribute anything to the substantive debate over the value or representativeness of aggressive regulation.

Nonetheless, a systematic empirical analysis of the policy consequences of a stronger legislative presence in implementation will make it more difficult to maintain the wide variety of conflicting expectations compared above. As the reader is now aware, new mechanisms of legislative control have been advocated as a cure for bad draftsmanship of administrative regulations, a method for counteracting special interest influence, a check on bureaucratic extremism, and an access opportunity for the unorganized citizenry. It is possible that the new mechanisms can have each of these effects in different circumstances or contexts. However, determining which effects (if any) are predominantly associated with legislative participation will help to resolve a number of broader questions about legislative behavior and the policy process, while also contributing information useful to those currently considering adoption of new control mechanisms.

NOTES

1. The most extreme statement of this view is associated with the New Public Administration. See H. George Frederickson, New Public Administration (University, Ala.: University of Alabama Press, 1980).

2. See Arthur E. Bonfield, "The Iowa Administrative Procedure Act: Background, Construction, Applicability, Public Access to Agency Law, the Rule-Making Process," Iowa Law Review, Vol. 60 (1975), p. 846.

3. Perhaps the best argument along these lines is that of Carl J. Friedrich, in "Public Policy and the Nature of Administrative Responsibility," Public Policy, Vol. 1 (1940), pp. 3-24.

4. Aaron Wildavsky, The Politics of the Budgetary Process, 2d ed. (Boston: Little, Brown, 1974).

5. Ibid., chs. 6-7.

6. Ibid. See also Emmette Redford, Democracy in the Administrative State (New York: Oxford University Press, 1969).

7. Although paradoxical in light of his work on the budgetary process, Wildavsky's coauthored work on implementation supports this conclusion. See Jeffrey Pressman and Aaron Wildavsky, Implementation, 2d ed. (Berkeley: University of California Press, 1979).

5

AN EMPIRICAL ANALYSIS

The previous chapters have explored the possible connections between a stronger legislative presence in implementation and certain important, identifiable policy consequences. Despite the polemical nature of much of the theorizing, verifiable research propositions can be constructed on the basis of the arguments advanced. This chapter is devoted to an empirical assessment of an essential form of legislative participation in implementation in an effort to resolve some of the uncertainty regarding its effects.

PREVIOUS EMPIRICAL RESEARCH

The primary objectives of initial research efforts in a new area are to provide background information and to suggest questions for further inquiry. A good portion of the previous research on committee review of administrative rule-making has unfortunately failed in these respects, sacrificing analytic clarity for either biased advocacy or legal hand-wringing.[1] However, a few studies have attempted to identify trends and relationships relevant to the present effort. A brief examination of some of these studies will help to establish the basis for the analysis to follow.

Glendon Schubert's study of legislative committee rule review in Michigan, published nearly a quarter of a century ago, was the first notable effort by a political scientist to examine this form of legislative participation in implementation.[2] Then, as now, many advocates of the mechanism argued that it would lead to a legislative equivalent of judicial review, creating a narrow, objective check on the legal integrity of administrative decisions. Schubert's investigation supported his conclusion that, contrary to these views, legislative review inevitably becomes "political" in practice.[3] His research thus established a basis for further analysis of the policy impact of the new legislative role. However, because Michigan's innovation was not emulated significantly until recently, Schubert's analysis remained relatively obscure.

One of the first political science studies of the current movement toward legislative committee rule review focused on legislator assessments of oversight efforts and effectiveness.[4] William Lyons and Larry Thomas surveyed legislators in Florida, Missouri, and Tennessee regarding their impressions of the oversight activities of their respective assemblies, each of which had adopted different approaches to the problem of rule review. While legislator attitudes varied within each state as a function of interest in oversight and other factors, Lyons and Thomas found significant interstate differences, leading them to conclude that "structure is clearly the dominant variable" in accounting for differences in the perceived effectiveness of oversight.[5] This conclusion adds support to research efforts (such as this one) that are based on the assumption that structural variations in legislative-administrative relations do make a difference in behavior, and perhaps in policy.

Much of the comparative state research has been devoted to analysis of the patterns of adoption of committee rule review mechanisms. In another 1979 study, Keith Hamm and Roby Robertson found that the states adopting committee rule review had legislatures that ranked relatively high in capability and governors who were relatively weak in formal powers.[6] It could be argued that these findings indicate that committee rule review is indeed a part of an overall legislative resurgence, since it has been adopted initially where legislatures apparently are in a strong position vis-à-vis the executive. However, Hamm and Robertson also found that states with committee rule review had relatively large administrative structures (in terms of the number of agencies in the state government) and, interestingly, the legislatures in these states spent a relatively low number of days in session.[7]

Although the relationships were not very strong, the Hamm and Robertson findings are generally consistent with the basic assumptions of the present research. The legislatures adopting committee rule review had well-developed staff and other resources, but they did not spend as much time in session as some other, less developed legislatures. A shift toward expanded participation in implementation at the expense of involvement in formulation may be indicated by this finding. The fact that these legislatures had created a relatively large number of agencies suggests that they had delegated considerable powers to administrators, a factor also consistent with such an interpretation.

The adoption patterns do not, however, provide any direct indication of the policy consequences of expanded legislative involvement in administrative decision-making. Figure 5.1 indicates which states had adopted committee rule review or sunset by 1979. The pattern is strikingly unlike the emulation pattern that has characterized major innovations in welfare, health, education, administrative organization, and other areas used by Walker in constructing his well-known index of innovativeness.[8] In fact, there is a disproportionate tendency for southern states to have adopted these mechanisms.[9]

This adoption pattern may be taken as confirmation of several contradictory propositions. Some may argue that legislative committee rule review and sunset have been adopted widely in the South because the policy subsystems of business interests and agreeable regulators are weaker there (because the industrial base is weaker) and thus unable to defeat the reform movement toward a stronger legislative presence in implementation. This line of reasoning assumes that the new legislative role is, as was argued in Chapter 2, a "progressive" expression of the public interest. Conversely, the pattern may be interpreted as a reflection of the conservative, antiregulatory political culture of the South, if one assumes that these legislative reforms are conservative in their policy impact.

In short, studying adoption patterns does not contribute significantly to resolution of the debate over the policy consequences of a stronger legislative role in implementation. The structural characteristics of committee rule review mechanisms may engender unintended consequences, making it possible that, whatever the intentions of their supporters, the mechanism may lead to greater or lesser regulatory aggressiveness. The policy impact of this form

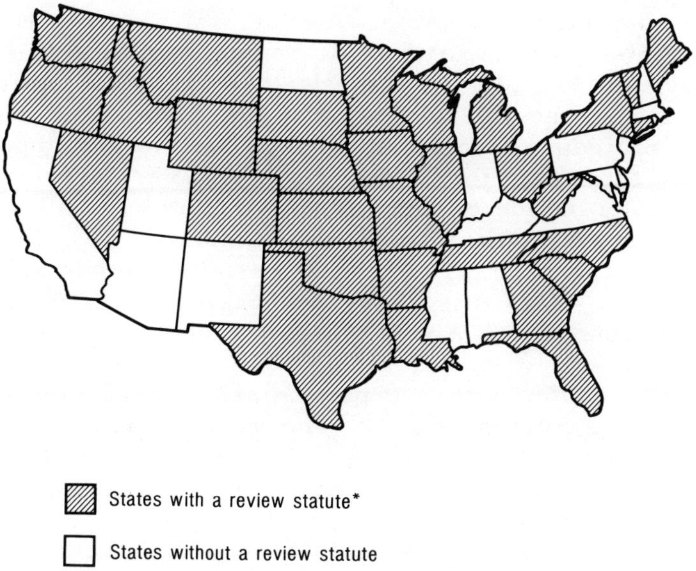

Source: Statute search as reported in R. Craig Williamson, "Legislative Review of Administrative Rules and Regulations: An Examination of State Procedures," paper presented at the Annual Meeting of the Southern Political Science Association, Memphis, November 5-7, 1981.

*Alaska is now included in this group of states.

Figure 5.1 State Statutes Establishing Legislative Committee Review of Administrative Regulations

of legislative participation remains an empirical question not resolved by analysis of the motives of those advocating it or of its adoption patterns.

A controversial but often-used approach for assessing the policy impact of a structural change is to compare the policies of states with it to those of states without it. Although such an approach would not include any direct observation of committee or agency action, it could serve as a useful preliminary inquiry. Using data from the mid-1970s, this writer undertook such a study in an effort to determine the effect of legislative committee rule review on the substance of environmental policy.[10]

The general conclusion of the study supports the position advocated in Chapter 3: the states with some form of legislative committee rule review had somewhat less aggressive air pollution standards than the other states.[11] (Interestingly, the relation between the adoption of administrative procedure reforms and policy was in the opposite [positive] direction; the states with the most elaborate requirements for notice of administrative hearings had somewhat more aggressive air pollution standards.[12]) This study did not explain much of the variation among the state pollution standards, however, making it difficult to reach firm conclusions about the policy effect of committee rule review.

Causal inferences are particularly tenuous when interpreting this kind of study. The mild inverse association between the presence of committee rule review statutes and regulatory aggressiveness may be entirely spurious. Most obviously, sluggish regulatory policy implementation and the enactment of the review statutes may both be reflections of generalized antibureaucratic attitudes.[13] Since the research simply determined the extent to which states with and without the review mechanism differed with respect to regulatory aggressiveness, it cannot be contended that the review mechanisms were ever used to achieve the more moderate pollution standards. A meaningful analysis of the policy impact of legislative participation in implementation requires that actual legislative behavior be observed and systematically evaluated.

The states chosen for this analysis (Georgia, Iowa, Michigan, Wisconsin, and Tennessee) represent a wide variety of social, economic, and political conditions. For example, these states cover a range from among the most "moralistic" to among the most "traditionalistic" on the Elazar-Sharkansky political culture scale, and from 3.81 to 5.78 on the well-known Walker innovativeness index.[14] They vary considerably with regard to population density, industrialization, per capita income, and region. While it cannot constitute a scientific sample of all 50 states, this group does provide the basis for important contributions to theory building, with obvious implications for the other states and even for Congress.

The case studies have three main parts. First, documents and statutes were studied in order to gain an understanding of the structural and legal foundations of legislative committee rule review in each state. Second, an extensive study of official records of committee actions on agency regulatory decisions was undertaken. The primary objective here was to determine systematically what kinds of policies and what kinds of agencies were most often the targets of legislative disapproval. The information obtained in this phase of the investigation provided data useful in determining the policy consequences of the mechanism as it works in practice. (Because of differences in data availability, this part of the study was more elaborate for Michigan, Tennessee, and Wisconsin than in the other two states.) Finally, semistructured interviews with agency officials, legislators, and committee staff provided useful insights regarding the motivations for committee action, administrative responses to (and anticipations of) such actions, and general assessments of the process. The following case studies are compared and evaluated more generally in Chapter 6.

MICHIGAN: LET'S KEEP EVERYBODY HAPPY

The Process

The Michigan Administrative Procedures Act of 1969, as amended (M.C.L. 24.201 et seq.), contains the current statutory provisions governing agency rule-making and legislative review. Figure 5.2 is a flow chart of the process, illustrating all possible consequences of committee action or inaction. Although much of the process is similar to that in other states, several points are noteworthy.

Agencies are required to hold public hearings on all proposed rules, including amendments and repeals, with the exception of emergency rules.[15] (While most states routinely require such public hearings, a few allow for promulgation of rules without public hearings when no groups or citizens petition for one after publication of the proposed rules.[16]) Michigan agencies are required to give public notice of the hearing at least ten days in advance, although most agency enabling statutes require 30 or more days' notice. The notice must be published as required by the agency enabling statute and also mailed to the Joint Committee on Administrative Rules, the governor, and "all persons who have requested . . . advance notice of proposed action which may affect them."[17] Staff assistants of the Joint Committee normally attend agency rule-making

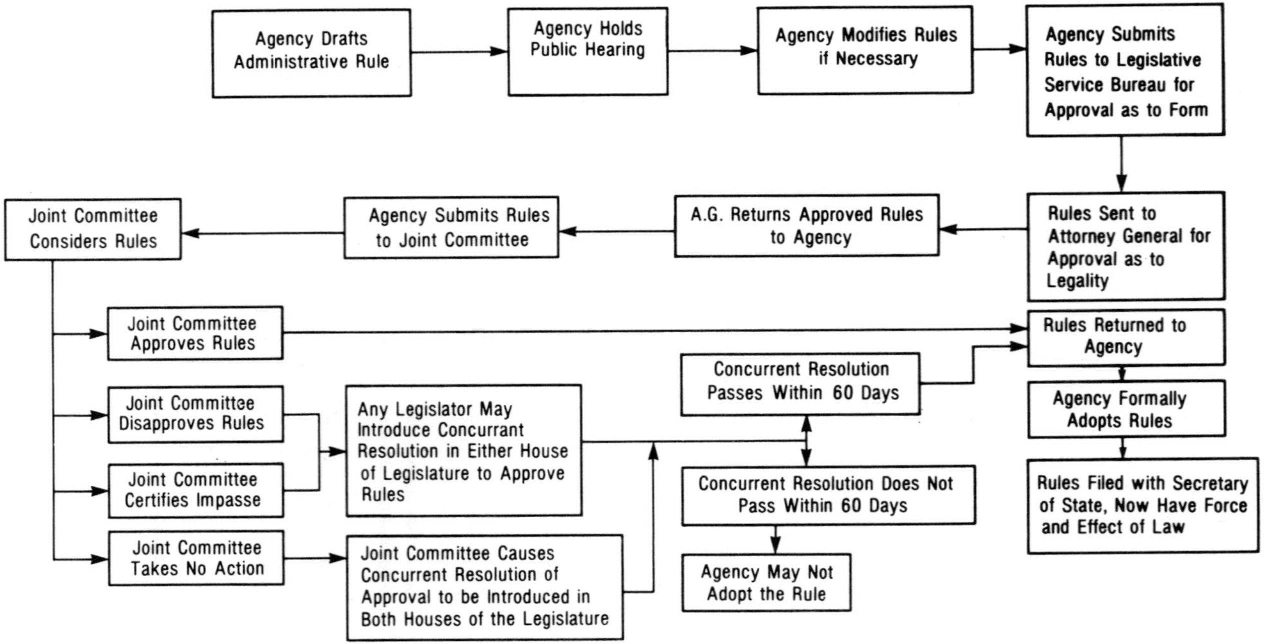

<u>Source</u>: Michigan Joint Committee on Administrative Rules, "Processing of Proposed Guidelines and Administrative Rules," mimeo, May 1979.

Figure 5.2 The Rule Review Process in Michigan

hearings to "audit" agency compliance with public participation requirements.

After the hearing, the agency submits final drafts of the rules to the Legislative Service Bureau for approval of their form and numbering. They are then sent to the attorney-general for approval with regard to consistency with existing statutes and constitutional provisions. Both reviews are largely perfunctory.

The agency submits its proposed rules to the Joint Committee only after all preliminary reviews are completed. Consequently, the committee only reviews rules that have already been the subject of at least one public hearing and have been approved by two other offices of state government. The agency must submit 35 copies of the rules to the Joint Committee, clearly identifying additions to and deletions from existing rules.

The rules must be accompanied by a report containing the following information:

> a concise statement of principal reasons for the rules;
> the names of persons connected with the agency and of persons outside the agency urging adopting of the rules;
> an analysis of the rules;
> all methods of notice of agency hearing on the rules including newspaper and other publications used;
> the time, place, length of hearing and approximate number of persons in attendance;
> the names of organizations and interests represented at the hearing, and names and titles of their representatives with complete addresses and a summary of their remarks;
> the major suggestions made at the hearing by organizations and answers thereto by agency representatives;
> the fiscal implications to the state and/or local units of government.[18]

The scope and detail of this required report is one of the most distinctive features of the Michigan rule review process. Any complaint or criticism regarding an administrative proposal voiced in formal agency proceedings must be forwarded to the Joint Committee along with information about the identity of those participating. Attendance at the hearings by the committee staff is designed to provide a check on the adequacy of the public hearing and the completeness of the agency's report. This requirement thus gives the committee not only new data on the advantages and disadvantages of the agency proposal, but also specific information about the support and opposition of important individuals and organizations.

The Joint Committee has two months in which to consider the agency proposals, although it can extend the period to three months when more time is considered necessary. The committee review process is normally set up on a monthly cycle with hearings scheduled for a few days of each month.

At the hearings, committee members listen to presentations by agency members and to private citizens and others who wish to present their views on the proposed rules. Additional input is provided by the committee staff, which frequently prepares an analysis of proposed rules expected to be controversial. These analyses are given to committee members prior to the hearings. Since the committee staff consists primarily of two attorneys, the written analyses emphasize the legal rather than the substantive aspects of the proposed rules. For example, one staff member indicated that he always directed the committee's attention to any "catch-all" categories in listings of prohibited activities in agency rules (for example, "any other unprofessional conduct" as grounds for suspension of a license). From a legal perspective, such provisions are unacceptably vague, and the committee consequently routinely objects to them. The staff report also includes detailed information on the agency rule-making hearings.

The committee has four options: approval, disapproval, certification of an impasse, and no action. All committee actions require not a simple majority of the ten members, but "concurring majorities of the members of the committee from each House." Since there are five members from each House, this provision makes it possible for a minority of either three House members or three Senate members to block committee action.

If the rules are approved, the agency may adopt and enforce them after they are filed with the Secretary of State. If the committee votes to disapprove a rule, the agency may not adopt it unless the entire legislature approves the rule by concurrent resolution or the committee formally reverses its vote and approves the rule. Thus, formal action by the committee with no involvement by the whole assembly can lead to immediate promulgation of the rules or to their immediate annulment.

The committee's third option, certification of an impasse, has the same effect as disapproval. Unless the committee subsequently approves it, a concurrent resolution of the whole legislature is necessary to approve a rule that has been the subject of a committee impasse. Similarly, if no committee action is taken, the rules cannot be promulgated unless a concurrent resolution of approval is passed, but such a resolution is automatically introduced by the committee after a no action decision when its time for review has expired. In response to committee objections, an agency may elect to withdraw a rule to make minor changes. The committee review then begins anew, with a full two-month consideration period beginning on the date of resubmission by the agency.

The Michigan legislature thus participates quite heavily in the rule-making process. Legislative staff monitor agency compliance with public participation requirements, and statutes require extensive reports of agency rule-making activities that occur before the rules reach the committee. The committee review process is designed to require positive action by a majority of both the House and Senate members of the committee in order that a rule be approved, and although committee action can be rescinded by a concurrent resolution of the legislature, no such resolution is required to affirm it. During the period studied, approximately one-third of the rules submitted were disapproved or withdrawn in face of committee objection or were the subject of a committee impasse.

Impact on Agency Decision-Making

Legislative review affects agency decision-making in Michigan primarily by significantly increasing the importance of complaints about regulatory policy voiced by the public. An official with the Department of Natural Resources (DNR) reported that the first question asked by a committee member at the rule review hearings is always "Was there any opposition or controversy regarding these rules at your public hearing?" An attorney with the Secretary of State's office (which recently promulgated controversial rules on registration of lobbyists) said that the committee was mainly interested in whether his office had "taken care of public concerns" raised at the hearing.

This interest in conciliating the public, while eminently understandable from a legislator's perspective, does not usually lead to careful analysis by the committee of new ways to approach a regulatory problem. The DNR officials reported that the committee usually takes no substantive stand on the matter at hand, simply directing the agency to "go back and reach a workable compromise" where controversy still exists. In fact, the most obvious regularity in committee discussions is a general predisposition to support agency decisions that can be reasonably interpreted as a good faith compromise between opposing viewpoints.[19]

A recent decision on ski regulations promulgated by the DNR illustrates this pattern.[20] A person who owned a cabin on a small lake wanted the DNR to prohibit all skiing on the lake because of the alleged disturbance it caused him. Boaters wanted unrestricted access to the lake for any and all purposes. The committee was satisfied with a compromise decision to regulate the hours in which skiing would be allowed. Although the cabin owner was not satisfied, the decision had the appearance of a good compromise and therefore was accepted. Committee members even scolded the recalcitrant party for refusing to meet the opposition "half way."

The committee's interest in avoiding or minimizing controversy is inevitably frustrating to administrators. Several agency officials complained that the enabling legislation on which their regulations were based was itself objectionable to certain segments of the public because it inherently required or prohibited certain activities. It is unavoidable, they argued, that their regulations would cause some public objection in these cases because the law itself mandated something opposed by those affected. The committee's practice of objecting to agency proposals that generate opposition thus leads several administrators to complain that they are being asked to do the impossible.

For example, the lobbyist registration law mentioned above was enacted at the behest of several public interest groups and had general public support. The law called for the Secretary of State to promulgate regulations defining the details of registration. When the regulations disturbed many lobbyists by requiring that they report travel costs incurred in "research," the committee objected to the rules. A State Department official complained that "there is simply no way to require meaningful lobbyist registration without making some lobbyists mad, and yet, that is what the committee apparently demands."[21]

The impact of committee rule review in Michigan serves to retard the resolution of difficult policy issues even within the legislature itself. A staff attorney with the Joint Committee, who is generally supportive of committee rule review, admitted that the availability of the mechanism has led legislators to enact increasingly vague legislation. When a particular issue is politically intractable, some legislators argue that a broad delegation is appropriate since later action through committee review is possible if agency decisions prove politically disruptive.[22]

Committee review has also been used to prevent administrative resolution of policy issues when it is attempted as a substitute for legislative enactment. A representative from the DNR reported that there was a strong movement for regulation of underwater salvage operations and that such regulation was urgently needed in light of increasing salvage activities taking place in the Great Lakes. The legislature, however, had been unable to pass a special bill for underground salvage regulation, reportedly because of an anti-DNR senator on a committee with jurisdiction over conservation matters. When the DNR decided to promulgate regulations under its existing mandates, the Joint Committee on Administrative Rules objected because of the lack of statutory authority, although the committee members favored the substance of the regulation. They simply felt that the matter should be addressed through legislation.[23]

It should be noted that committee review in Michigan has unearthed and corrected instances in which agency decisions have blatantly contradicted clearly expressed legislative intent. A committee staff member reported that the Commerce Department had acted in such a manner when it issued a recent regulation dealing with advertisement of franchise opportunities. The legislature, after exhaustive debate, had decided not to require that all advertisements of franchise opportunities include a lengthy caveat that would have doubled the length of the advertisement. The Commerce Department nonetheless included the caveat requirement in its regulations implementing the statute. Similar cases were reported involving rules proposed by the Public Service Commission and the Secretary of State.[24] In all these cases the Joint Committee quickly disapproved the agency proposals.

Of course, the present study is concerned with the policy effect of legislative committee rule review, a matter that transcends the more immediate legal issues. Even if most committee objections are based on sound legal reasoning, it is important to determine whether the cumulative impact of such objections affects policy implementation in a substantive sense. It is possible that not all legally sound objections are actually made, and, of course, it is often possible to make one of several contrasting objections all supported by legal justification. In short, legislative committee rule review may have policy effects irrespective of the legal status of committee actions. The next section is designed to explore this possibility.

A Quantitative Assessment

The ideal way to assess empirically the policy effect of committee rule review would be to use a quasiexperimental design that measures regulatory aggressiveness or stringency before and after the establishment of committee rule review powers. Assuming that contextual and historical factors could be accounted for, such an approach would provide a direct indication of the nature and extent of any policy effects. Unfortunately, the necessary data were not available in a meaningful and comparable form for this kind of analysis.

However, the propositions summarized in Chapter 4 can be empirically assessed through a systematic investigation of committee records. A comprehensive record of the formal decisions made by the Michigan Joint Committee on Administrative Rules was available that covered the period from November 1977 through July 1980. The record contains committee decisions on 375 rule submissions by a variety of administrative agencies.[25] Specifically, the record reveals the committee action, the name of the agency involved, an indication of the substance of the agency proposal, and the dates of submission and committee action. Information was not available on the grounds for committee objections, and thus, with the exception of the cases described in the previous section, there was no direct indication of the committee's policy objectives that may have been relevant to their decisions.

Nonetheless, the available information can be used to evaluate the arguments linking a stronger legislative presence in implementation to changes in regulatory aggressiveness. The validity of these arguments can be revealed, in part, by determining what factors are most important in predicting committee objections. Before specifying hypotheses and variables, it is necessary to show how each position leads to certain expectations regarding the predictability of committee oversight actions.

If committee rule review only improves the "legal soundness" of agency proposals, the committee actions will not follow a consistent pattern with regard to policy factors such as policy content or agency type. Moreover, if committee rule review addresses broader concerns but provides an access opportunity effectively open to all interests, individual committee decisions would be determined by the balance of political forces acting in each particular case, a balance that would not consistently favor one type of interest over another. Some disapprovals would favor aggressive regulation and some would favor opposing causes. Committee action would not be predictable because the many individual objections would be in response to diverse (and collectively representative) influences. Thus, both the pluralistic-accountability position and the position of those who expect committee rule review to perform a limited legal review imply that committee decisions will not be predictable by reference to the above types of information. In the aggregate, committee action should be random with respect to policy-related factors.

However, if committee rule review has a persistent effect on regulatory aggressiveness, committee action should not be random but should follow an identifiable pattern. The position described in Chapter 2--legislative participation facilitates regulatory aggressiveness--is based on the assumption that oversight mechanisms work to counteract the special linkages that are said to develop between regulator and regulated. These linkages are not expected to be equally strong for all agencies, since regulated groups share close professional, educational, and even personnel connections only with certain agencies--their subsystem partners. If we assume, as Lowi argues, that an authoritative oversight mechanism will detect bureaucratic deviation from legislative intent, and that the deviations of most concern are those that result from excessive influence by the regulated, then some agencies will encounter conspicuously more committee objections than others. In particular, the "regulatory" agencies (occupational licensing boards, for example), chronically subject to effective capture by the regulated, should constitute the primary focus of the reviewing committee's objections.

The position described in Chapter 3--legislative participation inhibits regulatory aggressiveness--assumes that interests opposing burdensome regulations are the primary beneficiaries of oversight mechanisms. While the Chapter 2 position emphasizes the political importance of a special type of bureau-client linkage, this position emphasizes the contrasting forums created by administrative hearings and legislative committee hearings. If certain elements of the latter create especially useful access opportunities for interests opposing aggressive regulations, committee objections will be directed toward agency proposals that contain unwanted restrictions or requirements, particularly those relating to business activity. And, since opponents of regulation are subject to burdensome restrictions and requirements imposed by many agencies (not only their subsystem partners), committee actions as predicted by this position will be taken against the restrictive proposals of any and all rule-making bureaus.[26]

It should be noted that this second proposition is asserted both by the planning-administrative opponents of a stronger legislative role and by those who support such a role on the basis of the conservative version of the legal-accountability position. They differ, of course, on the issue of whether regulated groups should have greater influence in regulatory policy implementation. However, the positions are identical with regard to the predictability of committee objections: the committee is expected to act most often when agencies propose restrictive or burdensome regulations.

In sum, these contrasting propositions can be empirically assessed by determining whether, and in what way, committee action can be predicted on the basis of certain policy-related variables. If rule review facilitates regulatory vigor, committee action should be <u>agency specific</u> (focusing on regulatory agencies). If it inhibits regulatory vigor, committee action should be <u>rule specific</u> (focusing on restrictive proposals). If it has no cumulative effect on policy, committee action will be equally likely for all agencies and for all types of proposals, and hence, unpredictable on the basis of the data available here.

Variables

Three independent variables were constructed on the basis of the available data in ways that will make it possible to detect any relevant patterns in committee action. The first variable, "agency type," is a simple trichotomy based on the major tasks and jurisdictions of agencies with rule-making authority. The categories reflect the varying degree to which regulation is the essential function of the agency. Thus, agencies were classified as "regulatory," "mixed," and "service." Although the classification is not unidimensional, it is treated as ordinal with respect to the purposes of this analysis, each agency receiving a score of 3, 2, or 1, corresponding to the extent to which its functions involve regulation. Nearly all of the agencies were unambiguously assigned to one of the categories, and the few uncertain classifications were resolved after discussion with a second observer.[27] Table 5.1 lists the agencies in each category.

The second variable, "rule restrictiveness," was constructed as a four-way classification of the subject matter content of agency proposals. Scores were assigned on the basis of a systematic content analysis with two coders making independent judgments. The coding process consisted of assigning a score of 1 to 4 based on the degree to which the agency proposal was perceived to involve restrictions or requirements burdensome to private activity. Once again, it is acknowledged that regulatory proposals vary in many respects, and that a unidimensional scale of rule restrictiveness is necessarily simplified. Nonetheless, it is appropriate for the present analysis inasmuch as restrictiveness is a variable attribute of regulatory aggressiveness. The categories are as follows:

Proposals relating to major aspects of private business activity	4
Proposals relating to minor aspects of private business activity	3
Proposals relating to regulation of private personal activity	2
Proposals relating to regulation of government personnel or procedures	1

Table 5.1 Designation of Agency Type

Regulatory (3)
Department of Natural Resources
Licensing and Regulatory Boards*
Department of Commerce
Civil Rights Commission
Mixed (2)
Department of Labor
Department of Agriculture
Department of Public Health
Department of State
Department of Transportation
Department of Mental Health
Service (1)
Department of Education
Office of Management and Budget
Attorney-General
Civil Service Commission
Department of the Treasury
Department of Social Services
State Police

*This includes a large number of relatively small boards, each charged with responsibility for regulating a specific profession.

The conceptual basis for the above categories was tied to the theoretical discussion presented earlier. "Regulatory aggressiveness" is a rather vague term, but its meaning in the context of Lowi's arguments and the alternative ideas is fairly definite. Regulated or clientele groups presumably oppose agency actions that could increase their operating costs or expenses, and these were scored 4 by the coders. When agency proposals were of this general type but were perceived to be less significant, they were placed in the next category. Regulations relating to "private personal activity" (for example, hunting regulations) could be considered relevant to regulatory stringency, but these are usually a lower priority for regulated or client groups. Finally, the lowest category was designed to include agency proposals that only affect agency operation or that are otherwise expected to be insignificant to organized interests. If, as the planning-administrative position predicts, legislative participation occurs primarily in response to complaints by regulated or client interests, committee objections will not be random with respect to this variable.

The coders assigned identical scores in slightly more than 60 percent of the cases, and disagreements were almost always over adjacent categories.[28] The actual calculations reported below were made on the basis of the average score given to each proposal by the coders. Thus, the rule restrictiveness variable had seven possible values (1, 1.5, 2, 2.5, 3, 3.5, 4) for computational purposes. For example, a proposal was scored 4 only if the coders agreed that it should receive the maximum score; it was scored 3.5 if one coder gave it a 3.

Finally, each agency was classified as either a "department" (such as Public Health, Transportation, Education) or an "agency" (such as the Barber Board). This dichotomy was included in order to distinguish between the large cabinet-level departments with presumably significant lobbying potential and the smaller agencies with presumably little lobbying potential. It was expected that this variable would help to explain some additional variation in committee action.

The dependent variable, committee action, consisted of only two categories, approval and disapproval. The disapproval category included not only proposals on which the committee voted disapprovals and formal objections, but also cases in which the agency withdrew its rules, along with those in which the committee reached an impasse. The common element among all these types of action is the probability that committee demands exerted some measure of influence on the final administrative action and its implementation.[29] The remaining proposals were placed in the approved category.

Thus, a set of empirical data was constructed in which regulatory proposals constituted the unit of analysis. A discriminant analysis was performed to determine if and in what manner the information on proposal content and bureau characteristics could predict committee action.

Findings

The discriminant function computed on the basis of the independent variables discussed above correctly predicted 62 percent of the committee actions. Rule restrictiveness was the primary predictor. The extent to which a bureau's activities involve regulation (agency type) did not appear to be related to the propensity for committee action. Table 5.2 reports the actual and predicted committee actions and ranks the independent variables with regard to the magnitude of the standardized discriminant function coefficients.

Table 5.2 Predicting Committee Rule Review in Michigan: Discriminant Function Analysis

		Predicted: Approved Proposals	Predicted: Disapproved Proposals
Actual:	Approved Proposals (N = 257)	159	98
	Disapproved Proposals (N = 107)	40	67
	Percent Correctly Predicted:	62	
	Correlation Between Discriminant Function and Discriminating Variables:		
	Rule Restrictiveness	.84	
	Agency Type	-.47	
	Department v. Agency	-.30	
	Canonical Correlation	.26	

The inability of the discriminant function to predict committee action with high accuracy indicates that other factors not included in this analysis are important in determining committee decisions. Nonetheless, it is clear the committee objections in Michigan are not random with regard to the restrictiveness of regulatory proposals.[30] A comparison of group means of approved and disapproved proposals provides a direct indication of the magnitude and direction of the effects of the independent variables (see Table 5.3). The proposals that encountered some form of legislative objection were significantly higher in restrictiveness than the approved proposals. The average disapproved proposal was scored 3.20 on the 4-point restrictiveness scale, while the average approved proposal was scored only 2.74. The data thus indicate that the Michigan rule review committee is considerably more likely to find something to criticize in regulatory proposals when they involve restrictions on private business activity than when they affect only personal actions or government operations.

Table 5.3 Comparison of Approved and Disapproved Agency Proposals in Michigan

Committee Action		Restrictiveness	Agency Type	Percent by Departments
Approved	(257)	2.74[a]	2.47	81[b]
Disapproved	(107)	3.20[a]	2.34	70[b]

[a]The difference between these means is significant at the .01 level.
[b]The difference between these means is significant at the .05 level.

Service, mixed, and regulatory agencies and departments were equally likely to encounter legislative objection. The only bureau characteristic related to committee action was department versus agency status; a disproportionately large number of the disapproved proposals were from the small agencies and boards. The major departments apparently fared somewhat better before the reviewing committee, although the difference is not large.

The findings add support to the idea that the reviewing committee is not primarily motivated by a neutral, objective concern for legal soundness in administrative regulation, since the chance of objection is noticeably greater when Michigan administrators propose restrictive regulatory changes. However, predictions based on the restrictiveness indicator are not highly accurate; many restrictive proposals are approved and many nonrestrictive proposals are disapproved. Some of the difficulty of prediction may be attributed to the imprecise variable construction necessitated by the available data. Better measurement would probably improve the discriminating power of the variable. Nonetheless, analysis of the residual or mispredicted cases may provide additional information useful in assessing the propositions.

The mispredicted cases were considered in order to determine if any patterns could be detected that could account for the unclear connection between rule restrictiveness and committee action. Two kinds of mispredicted cases were possible: false disapprovals (proposals that were incorrectly predicted to encounter objection) and false approvals (proposals incorrectly predicted to obtain approval). There were 98 false disapprovals and 40 false approvals. Since the rule restrictiveness variable was the primary basis for prediction, false disapprovals can be generally interpreted as cases in which relatively restrictive proposals were approved, and false approvals can be generally interpreted as cases in which relatively nonrestrictive proposals were disapproved.

The residual analysis produced one striking finding: the greatest number of false disapprovals were proposals from occupational licensing boards.[31] Nearly 24 percent of the false disapprovals were proposals from these agencies, although they contributed only 13 percent of the total proposals. The false approvals did not reveal such a clear pattern, except that the Department of Natural Resources was the most represented rulemaker in this group. The occupational licensing boards encountered objection when approval was predicted only four times during the two-and-one-half years covered by the analysis.

The tendency of the reviewing committee to treat restrictive proposals from occupational licensing boards with special favor suppressed the explanatory power of the discriminant function. With all the proposals from these boards omitted from the analysis, the independent variables predicted committee action with considerably greater accuracy: over 67 percent of the remaining cases were correctly predicted.

The fact that proposals from occupational licensing boards were approved by the reviewing committees despite their apparently restrictive content adds considerable weight to the proposition that committee action inhibits regulatory aggressiveness. Restrictive proposals from occupational licensing boards, typically intended to restrict entry into a profession in order to protect those licensed from competition, are conspicuously successful in obtaining committee approvals. However, those opposing regulations that are actually burdensome to the regulated are apparently able to find a favorable audience in the rule review committee. The findings thus suggest that the reviewing committee commonly disapproves restrictive pollution regulations and burdensome recordkeeping requirements, for example, but that it is not normally opposed to regulations raising minimum standards for entering licensed professions, a restriction often actively sought by the regulated. In short, committee rule review appears to be especially responsive to regulated and client groups.

Conclusion

Michigan's legislative rule review process is not steered by an ideological commitment. The perspective that is most important in guiding the decisions of its reviewing committee is simply a concern for the political satisfaction aspects of administrative decisions. Consequently, the legislators participating in implementation through this process do not regularly analyze the substance of regulatory actions, but typically focus upon the degree and sources of opposition to them.

Nonetheless, the data indicate that this method for expanding the legislative role in implementation is not neutral with regard to the substance of regulatory policy. Even without a developed ideological position, the reviewing committee's objections tend to follow a pattern supportive of the interests of regulated groups. Not only are burdensome regulations more likely to be disapproved than other agency proposals, but the agencies with the greatest success rate before the committees are the occupational licensing boards, normally considered more susceptible to capture by regulated groups than other units of state administration. The fact that they encounter such a low proportion of committee objections--even when proposing restrictive rules--indicates that the actions, if not the explicit motivations, of the reviewing committee members tend to inhibit aggressive regulation.

Of course, the Michigan Joint Committee on Administrative Rules does not always object to burdensome regulations, and the data do not indicate such a one-sided result. There is nothing in the structure of rule review in Michigan or even in the views of important legislators to prevent the committee from responding to pressures for aggressive regulation at the behest of public advocates or the general public. However, there are good reasons to conclude that, whatever the cause, legislative involvement in this aspect of the implementation process provides an access opportunity especially useful to the regulated.

TENNESSEE: POLITICS AS USUAL

The Process

Legislative committee participation in agency decisionmaking has changed substantially in Tennessee since its controversial beginnings in 1975. The original process was, in formal terms, one of the most radical of all those in effect at the time. The secretary of state was directed to transmit copies of all new rules, amendments, or repeals to the speakers of each house of the General Assembly when officially filed. The respective speakers then assigned these to the appropriate standing committees. If either standing committee voted to suspend an agency decision, the rule, amendment, or repeal became null and void when the objection was filed with the secretary of state. Committee actions could be rescinded by a joint resolution of the General Assembly, but such a resolution was not necessary to confirm or finalize any suspension.[32]

The constitutionality of this process was questioned vehemently by the attorney-general and the governor, the latter promising to "ignore" any committee objections to agency decisions.[33] The initial controversy was largely confined to matters of legal principle, however, because the mechanism was almost never used. In fact, the only two instances of committee objection that occurred under this early system were not even good test cases. The first suspension involved a Revenue Department regulation that provided for a sales tax on eyeglasses sold by ophthalmologists. The Senate Commerce and Labor Committee voted a suspension in response to a number of complaints by disgruntled consumers. However, the Revenue Department contended, with an attorney-general's opinion for support, that the rule in question simply restated applicable statutory provisions, and that the tax would still be collected even if the rule were suspended. The General Assembly then amended the statute.[34]

The other case involved strip-mining rules proposed by the Department of Conservation. After the department presented its case to the Senate General Welfare and Environmental Committee, the decision to suspend was indefinitely postponed. The rules were then voluntarily retracted by the department. No official action was ever taken by the committee.[35]

It became clear that no systematic review activity was likely under this arrangement. The law created new authority but it did not establish a new reviewing structure. The standing committees were simply inundated with volumes of agency regulations, the bulk of which were highly detailed and noncontroversial. They were normally ignored by the standing committees, their members continuing to spend most of their time on legislation and constituent service.

The obvious inadequacy of this system led to structural changes beginning in 1977, which eventually led to the establishment of a special oversight process. By 1978 the Goverment Operations Committees of both the House and Senate received all proposed rules, holding monthly hearings to consider and review them. The House and Senate versions of the committees were merged in 1981, creating the Joint Committee on Government Operations. In addition to rule review, this committee also has authority to perform evaluations associated with the sunset program.

Agencies are required to furnish "rule summaries" when proposing new rules, repeals, or amendments. This report was initially prepared by the agencies in any manner they considered appropriate. However, in 1980 the Administrative Procedures Division of the secretary of state's office (a legislatively controlled office in Tennessee) developed formal guidelines for the reports. Although not as comprehensive as Michigan's, the Tennessee reporting system requires the agency to summarize the proposals and to indicate which "persons, corporations, municipalities, or government units" will be affected. It is notable that, as in Michigan, Tennessee administrators must indicate the "names of persons and organizations . . . outside the agency urging adoption or rejection" of the proposal. The legislative staff adds its own analysis to the report.[36]

The legislature receives the agency proposals only after they have been the subjects of an administrative rule-making hearing or after they have been officially published as proposed rules giving interested parties the opportunity to petition for a hearing. The attorney-general also performs a perfunctory review of statutory authority before the proposals are sent to the legislature. The joint committee has 45 days in which to review them.

If no action is taken during this period the rules are considered approved, to become effective after filing with the secretary of state. The committee is empowered to disapprove agency proposals only if they are "illegal, unreasonable, or contrary to legislative intent."[37] If a disapproval is contemplated, notice must be given to the agency in question at least 15 days in advance of the hearing in which the action may be taken. Any committee action can be rescinded by passage of a joint resolution. During the period studied, approximately one-sixth of the agency proposals were either disapproved or subjected to a disapproval hearing.

Impact on Agency Decision-Making

The actual process of committee review in Tennessee is largely dependent upon forces outside the legislature. Although every rule submission is formally subject to legislative review, the real review does not take place until after a "notice of disapproval hearing" has been given by the committee. There is no regularized pattern of reviewing all rule submissions in the presence of agency representatives, the latter being required to meet with the committee only when disapproval is being considered. The process is thus unlike Michigan's in which objections raised in agency rule-making hearings are routinely discussed along with staff analyses of agency proposals in a meeting with the rule-making officials.

The selectivity of the legislative rule review process in Tennessee is perhaps its most notable characteristic. The fact that it takes relatively few formal actions reduces its general level of visibility.[38] Its proceedings are rarely covered by the press, and attendance is normally limited to staff members and officials from other agencies. In a recent interview, a member of the Administrative Procedures Division who staffs the committee asserted that, as a result of its selectivity and low visibility, the review process in Tennessee is the most explicitly political review process in his experience.[39]

Before assessing the policy implications of the process through a quantitative analysis, a description of a few cases may help to describe the manner in which rule review operates. In 1977 the commissioner of the Alcoholic Beverage Commission solicited an opinion from the attorney-general regarding the constitutionality of the commission's prohibition--through administrative rule--of liquor price advertising.[40] An opinion was handed down in March of that year, which held that although the commission had the power to regulate advertisements and even announcements of price in certain circumstances, the blanket prohibition of price advertising was an infringement of the First Amendment.[41]

The commission considered the idea of repealing its prohibition of price advertising for over two years. On June 13, 1979, it gave official notice that public hearings would be held to consider a proposed repeal. According to the commissioner, all of the public comments at the hearing were supportive of the change. The organizations participating were mostly consumer groups and others contending that price advertisements would increase competition among retailers and thus lead to lower retail prices. The retail liquor association was conspicuously absent from the public hearing.[42]

The commission voted to repeal the rules prohibiting price advertisements. The repeal was not promulgated, however, until January 1980, being scheduled for legislative committee review in February. The committee delayed action until March 11. At that time, a notice of disapproval hearing was given, directing the commission to present reasons that the repeal should not be disapproved. The matter was continued until May 13, when it was formally disapproved by a 12-2 margin. The retail liquor association's chief lobbyist, well-known around the capitol, did attend the committee's hearings. Although price advertising was eventually permitted by later action in 1981, the committee rule review process delayed it for a considerable period.

The policy impact of legislative participation in this case was clear and direct. There was no concern for the integrity of previous legislative intent or for administrative compliance with proper legal standards (in fact, it appeared that the agency had been attempting to bring its regulations in line with constitutional provisions). Legislative review served as an access point for a regulated group that opposed an administrative decision that presumably would have served a broader interest.[43]

Two other notable examples do not reflect such an obvious legislative role in representing regulated interests over those of consumers and the general public, but the results are essentially in the same direction. The Tennessee Air Pollution Control Board proposed new regulations in the fall of 1979 that, among other things, would have classified two industrial sites as "nonattainment" areas. Such a classification would have prohibited plant expansions while requiring the installation of air pollution control devices on a Union Carbide plant.[44] At the committee hearings, Union Carbide, with the support of the Tennessee Manufacturers Association, argued that the regulations would force a plant shutdown, leading to extensive layoffs. The Air Pollution Control Board contended that the regulations would require only "minimal" costs. After delaying action for many months, the legislative rule committee disapproved the proposed rules.[45]

Proposed rules of the Revenue Department were disapproved after the reviewing legislators were persuaded that they would be "unduly" onerous to the regulated. The Revenue Department proposed rules that would have forced retail businesses to include charges for supplemental services (tailoring, consultation, and the like) in computation of their gross income for purposes of determining sales taxes. Several retail and labor organizations opposed the regulations and the committee disapproved them.[46]

Other examples indicate that rule review in Tennessee can work in other ways. The reviewing committee once objected to an Alcoholic Beverage Commission rule that would have expanded the amount of liquor that could be used for personal consumption by employees and owners of liquor stores. The existing regulations allowed eight cases of fifths per month to be allocated for this purpose by each store. The legislature felt that expanding the limit would only lead to bootleg sales and avoidance of state liquor taxes. An Education Department rule that would have required the use of stronger seat bolts in school buses was disapproved after it was argued that the existing bolts were adequate and new ones would only waste taxpayers' money.[47]

It is dangerous to make inferences about the political or policy impact of a form of influence on the basis of a few notable instances in which it has been used. Cogent arguments can be made to support both the agencies and the reviewing committees in all the cases discussed above. It is important to determine if committee decisions follow a persistent pattern of disproportionate representation of any given set of interests. The next section addresses this issue.

A Quantitative View

A comprehensive record of the action of the Tennessee rule review committees (House and Senate Committees on Government Operations through December 1980; Joint Committee on Government Operations thereafter) was available that covered the period January 1979 through May 1981, during which 243 agency proposals were considered. In addition to the record of committee action, copies of the Tennessee Administrative Register covering the period studied were available. Notices of proposed agency action were contained in this publication, indicating whether the rules were to be the subject of a public hearing or, as discussed above, to be promulgated after a suitable period passed after publication of the proposed rules without a proper petition for a hearing being submitted. Thus, the data set reveals: the committee action; the name of the agency involved; an indication of the substance of the agency proposal; the dates of submission and committee action; and an indication of whether the proposed rules had been the subject of an administrative rule-making hearing.

The same variables and methods used in analysis of the Michigan data were used with these data. Discriminant analysis was employed to determine if committee action could be predicted on the basis of the content of agency regulations and the type of agency proposing them. Once again, if legislative participation in implementation facilitates regulatory aggressiveness, we should expect that committee action is agency specific (focusing on regulatory agencies), and if it inhibits regulatory vigor, committee action should be rule specific (focusing on restrictive proposals). If committee actions are essentially random with respect to these variables, we can conclude that committee action is cumulatively neutral or that it only occurs in response to idiosyncratic legal deficiencies in agency proposals.

Agency type, rule restrictiveness, and agency versus department status were all constructed in the manner described in the section on Michigan. The coders agreed on approximately 60 percent of the coding decisions on rule restrictiveness, about the same level of agreement that was obtained with the Michigan data.[48] Analysis of the Tennessee data included one other variable, however: the presence or absence of a public hearing.

Both formal disapprovals and notices of disapproval hearings were included in the disapproved category of the committee action (dependent) variable. It was assumed that the committee exerted some influence in those cases in which it held a disapproval hearing, since such hearings require the agency to either justify its position or to change its proposals.

Findings

The results were strikingly similar to those found with the Michigan data. The discriminant function predicted committee action with somewhat greater accuracy (68 percent), but the other results were almost identical. Rule restrictiveness was by far the best predictor. The proposals that encountered some form of legislative opposition were significantly higher in restrictiveness than the other proposals, 3.15 as compared with 2.64. Thus, the Tennessee rule review committee, like its counterpart in Michigan, is considerably more likely to object to agency proposals when they involve restrictions on private business activity (see Tables 5.4 and 5.5).

The other variables also revealed similarities when compared with the Michigan findings. Service, mixed, and regulatory agencies were equally likely to encounter objection, but small agencies were somewhat more likely to encounter objection than the departments. The decision to hold a rule-making hearing instead of merely publishing proposed rules and holding a hearing only upon petition affects the likelihood of committee action. Administrative

Table 5.4 Predicting Committee Rule Review in Tennessee: Discriminant Function Analysis

		Predicted: Approved Proposals	Predicted: Disapproved Proposals
Actual:	Approved Proposals (N = 197)	132	65
	Disapproved Proposals (N = 34)	10	24

Percent Correctly Predicted:	68
Correlation Between Discriminant Function and Discriminating Variables:	
Rule Restrictiveness	.70
Agency Type	-.32
Department v. Agency	.03
Presence of Hearing	-.50
Canonical Correlation	.22

Table 5.5 Comparison of Approved and Disapproved Agency Proposals in Tennessee

Committee Action	Restrictiveness	Agency Type	Percent by Departments	Presence of Hearing
Approved (197)	2.64*	2.13	60	62*
Disapproved (34)	3.15*	2.14	50	47*

*The differences between these means is significant at the .05 level or better.

hearings had been held in connection with 62 percent of the approved agency proposals, but in only 47 percent of those disapproved (difference significant at the .05 level). Previous public exposure apparently decreases the probability of committee disapproval.

The accuracy of prediction, while higher than for the Michigan data, is still not very high, making residual analysis appropriate. The mispredicted cases were considered to determine, as in the previous section, if any patterns could be detected. There were 65 false disapprovals and 10 false approvals. The former can be generally interpreted as cases in which relatively restrictive proposals were approved, while the latter can be generally interpreted as cases in which relatively nonrestrictive proposals were disapproved.

The findings revealed the same pattern as was found in the Michigan residuals, except that it was even more pronounced in the Tennessee data. Over 35 percent of the false disapprovals were from the occupational licensing boards, although these boards contributed only 17 percent of the total proposals. Moreover, the occupational licensing boards were not represented even once among the false approvals. The data thus indicate that while restrictive agency proposals normally encounter a notably higher level of legislative opposition than other proposals, occupational licensing boards are able to obtain legislative approval even when their proposals are restrictive. As in Michigan, the reviewing committees have a strong propensity to make decisions that presumably favor regulated and client interests.

Conclusion

The results of the quantitative and impressionistic analyses reported here are consistent with the conclusions of a recent exhaustive study of Tennessee's rule review system by R. Craig Williamson.[49] His investigation noted that the process is surprisingly low in visibility (it is not regularly covered in either of the major Nashville newspapers), and that lobbying by special interests is made more effective as a result.[50] It is rare for an effective lobbying group to fail to obtain a satisfactory decision from the rule review committee.

Tennessee regulatory policy is probably less aggressive as a consequence of this form of legislative participation in implementation. If true, it is not clear that such a result is inevitable, however, because the reviewing committee appears to be able to respond to a variety of influences. The data merely indicate, with some consistency, that legislative objections are usually directed toward restrictive regulatory proposals unless they happen to be from occupational licensing boards. Strong public pressure, or even clear objective data (as in the case of the school bus seat bolts), can lead legislators to promote broader public interests with their decisions.

Nonetheless, the data suggest that regulated groups are normally more successful than others in influencing rule review decisions. The example of the Alcoholic Beverage Commission price advertising rule adds support to the argument, developed in Chapter 3, that such a result is ultimately a function of the fundamentally different access opportunities created by administrative hearings and committee rule review hearings. The regulated interests in that case clearly focused upon the latter in their efforts to influence policy implementation. There are strong indications that patterns of influence in regulatory policy are regularly affected in this direction by the availability of committee rule review.

WISCONSIN: VIRTUE THROUGH COMPLEXITY

The Process

Legislative review of administrative regulation in Wisconsin is quite complex when compared with the other states studied. Most important, Wisconsin has adopted a two-tier process in which standing committees and a special Joint Committee for Review of Administrative Rules (JCRAR) have suspension powers. Objections from the regular standing committees in each house must be supported by later JCRAR action in order to have permanent legal effect. Under this structure, nearly 5 percent of the proposed administrative regulations were rejected by standing committees and another 28 percent were modified to meet committee objections during the period studied. The JCRAR concurred in only about half of the formal objections. Thus, if this system of legislative participation in implementation has a significant policy effect, it must be attributable to the modifications in agency proposals obtained by the regular standing committees and to the threat of objection by these committees.

The establishment of legislative committee rule review in Wisconsin has been gradual, beginning in 1955 with the creation of JCRAR. The committee was quite inactive for many years, even after 1965 statutory changes supplemented its advisory authority with the power to suspend agency rules by a two-thirds vote. Amendments in 1973 allowed the committee to suspend rules by majority vote. The last amendments were enacted in 1979, establishing the process as it now exists.

As in the other states, the Wisconsin legislature is not involved in rule-making until after the agency has held public hearings on the proposed rules and after a technical review by the Legislative Council staff has been completed. This latter review is more extensive and less perfunctory than in other states, however. The council reviews agency rules to determine if proper statutory authority exists and to ensure that the rules are in the proper form, but it also investigates potential conflict with or duplications of existing rules. The grammar and clarity of the agency proposals are also reviewed. In 1980 the Legislative Council staff challenged 14 rule submissions for conflict with or duplication of existing rules, and it requested revisions of 161 rule submissions to improve clarity and grammar.

After clearing this hurdle, the agency submits its rules in final form to the presiding officer of each house of the legislature, who then sends the rules to a standing committee. The standing committees have 30 days in which to review the rules. Negotiation between one or both standing committees and the agency frequently takes place at this point. The committees may elect to hold public hearings on the rules, but a hearing is not required.

If the negotiation is unsuccessful and one of the committees remains unsatisfied, a formal objection is submitted by the committee to the JCRAR, which has 30 more days in which to review the objection. The JCRAR often acts as a referee at this point, managing additional negotiations between the objecting committee and the agency. If JCRAR officially nonconcurs with the standing committee's objection, the agency may promulgate the regulations. If it concurs, JCRAR must introduce a bill to support the objection in both houses. The agency may not promulgate the rules unless this bill fails.

JCRAR is also empowered to hold its own public hearings "to investigate complaints" regarding agency proposals that have not met with standing committee objections.[51] It may suspend the rule by an affirmative vote of a majority of the members present, in which case bills supporting the objection must be introduced in both houses. If the bills to support JCRAR's objection (whether or not a standing committee was initially involved) are introduced near the end of a legislative session or when the assembly is not in session, the agency proposals in question remain suspended until the next session.

Impact on Agency Decision-Making

Popular expectations regarding the policy impact of legislative committee rule review in Wisconsin were largely consistent with the views expressed in Chapter 3. Both supporters and opponents of the mechanism felt that the aggressiveness of public regulation would be reduced. Two important public advocate lobbies--Wisconsin's Environmental Decade, Inc., and the Center for Public Representation--were outspoken opponents of the new legislative review process. The environmental group even sued JCRAR on the grounds that its review powers were unconstitutional.[52]

Supporters of rule review had a wholly different perspective on what they wanted from government, but they agreed with the public advocates that it would help to moderate administrative regulation. Prior to an anticipated veto struggle over the rule review process, a Milwaukee general contracting firm sent a "Legislative Bulletin" to other firms urging them to support the legislative effort to override the governor's veto. The first line of the bulletin clearly revealed this firm's view of the purpose of legislative oversight: "Have you had enough rules and regulations proposed by state bureaucrats? Are you convinced state agencies are out of control. . . ?"[53] Committee rule review was hailed as a way to constrain administrative aggressiveness.

The Wisconsin legislative review process has not lived up to the expectations of either the pro- or antiregulatory forces. Certainly the number of regulations has not fallen. Nearly 250 rule submissions were received by the legislature in 1980, approximately the same number promulgated during recent previous years. Moreover, there are no obvious indications that the rule review process has resulted in a substantive shift in the direction of regulation policy.

Several examples illustrate this conclusion. First, the Labor Committee of the General Assembly (lower house) objected to a rule proposed by the Department of Industry, Labor, and Human Relations that would have set minimum wages for golf caddies and educational camp workers. A Senate committee also attempted to file an objection, but the motion failed on a tie vote. In both committees, the basis of the objection was concern about the potential economic hardships the rule would cause for those subject to the regulation.

JCRAR held a public hearing on January 4, 1980, to consider the objection. According to its report, no one registered at the hearing in support of the standing committee's objection, but 18 persons registered to oppose it. JCRAR voted 8-1 to nonconcur with the committee decision, and the new rules were promulgated.[54]

A second example followed the same pattern. On August 26, 1980, the Assembly Agriculture Committee objected to two Agriculture Department rules governing handwashing facilities on dairy farms and milk-cooling standards. In both cases, the proposed regulations would have brought Wisconsin dairies into conformity with the Pasteurized Milk Ordinance (PMO), a model dairy ordinance issued by the U.S. Public Health Service. The department and other supporters of the rules contended that Wisconsin statutes require that current regulations "be in reasonable accord" with recommendations of the U.S. Public Health Service, and that continued sales of Wisconsin dairy products to other states necessitated adoption of the more stringent regulations.

The Assembly Agriculture Committee was, nonetheless, persuaded that the rules would place an excessive financial hardship on producers of dairy products and that interstate sales would not decline if the old standards were maintained. JCRAR voted 5-4 and 6-3 to nonconcur with the objections, and the new standards were promulgated.[55]

The final example concerned an administrative rule setting a maximum limit on premiums for credit life insurance. Allegedly, the loss ratios of major credit life insurers were approximately half of what they should have been according to state law. The premiums normally charged resulted in a one-to-four ratio between claims and premiums, indicating that consumers were being overcharged by over $10 million per year.[56] To correct this imbalance, the state insurance commissioner proposed a rule reducing the maximum rate the companies charge for credit life insurance from $.60 to $.40 for every $100 of insurance. The change was designed to bring the loss ratios up to legal limits.

The administrative rule was submitted to the legislature in March 1981. After public hearings in July, both the Senate and Assembly Insurance Committees voted to object to the rule. The vote was 2-1 in the Senate Committee and 8-0 in the Assembly Committee. The latter asked the insurance commissioner to modify the rule, but he refused. The objections were submitted to JCRAR on July 27. After some deliberation, JCRAR reported nonconcurrence with the objections by an 8-0 vote on August 19. The Insurance Department regulation was upheld.[57]

These three examples contrast sharply with those in Michigan and Tennessee. Rule review, at least when the process reaches JCRAR, does not appear to have provided an effective means for the regulated to moderate regulation. JCRAR has repeatedly upheld administrative decisions even when strong political resistance has surfaced. Moreover, JCRAR even prompts agencies to stricter regulations on some occasions. Chairperson David Berger reported an instance in 1973 in which JCRAR forced the Department of Industry, Labor, and Human Relations to adopt a stricter fire code. The statute in question required sprinklers in all new buildings over 60 feet high, but the department's regulations had made sprinklers optional. Berger's JCRAR forced the department to change its regulations.[58]

As a result of its many proagency decisions, JCRAR has surprised many of its early critics. The public advocates who initially feared JCRAR as an access opportunity exclusively supportive of the regulated have now turned out to be the committee's strongest supporters. In particular, the Center for Public Representation has acclaimed JCRAR as an "effective forum for the debate of public issues."[59]

However, a review of notable cases does not reveal the typical effects of the process. As mentioned earlier, most legislative-administrative interaction with regard to administrative rules involves negotiation between agencies and regular substantive committees. Since agencies generally attempt to satisfy these committees, initial objections on their part can exert a significant effect on policy even when they do not culminate in formal JCRAR action. The following section addresses this possibility through quantitative analysis.

A Quantitative View

A comprehensive record of committee decisions on administrative regulations was available that covered all agency proposals considered during the 1981 legislative session (January-August). During this period, the committee considered 268 proposals, most of which were originally proposed during the session but others of which were proposed during the preceding year.

The record contained the same information contained in the Michigan record: the committee action and, in cases where the committee expressed dissatisfaction informally, an indication of whether the agency withdrew its proposal for modification; the name of the agency involved; an indication of the substance of the agency proposal; and the dates of submission and committee action.

The same variable construction and data analysis used in the two previous case studies were employed here. Discriminant analysis was used to determine if the committee's action was agency specific, rule specific, or random with regard to these factors. Agency type, rule restrictiveness, and agency versus department status were all constructed as described in the section on Michigan. However, the level of intercoder agreement on the content analysis of rule restrictiveness was somewhat higher; the coders assigned identical scores in 66 percent of the cases.[60] The higher level of agreement was probably due to the fact that the indication of the substance of the agency proposals was more complete than that for the other states.

Since the discriminant analysis was designed to detect patterns in formal or informal legislative influence exerted through rule review, the disapproved category of the dependent variable included cases in which agencies agreed to modify their proposals along with the few cases of formal objections.

Findings

The results were not consistent with those for Michigan and Tennessee. The discriminant function computed on the basis of the independent variables predicted only 56 percent of the cases correctly, and the approved and disapproved proposals were not significantly different with respect to any of the independent variables. However, it should be noted that rule restrictiveness was the best discriminating variable (although feeble), and that the direction of the relationship between this variable and committee action was consistent with the results for the other states. The disapproved proposals were slightly more restrictive than those approved without modifications being required (see Tables 5.6 and 5.7).

Table 5.6 Predicting Committee Rule Review in Wisconsin: Discriminant Function Analysis

		Predicted: Approved Proposals	Predicted: Disapproved Proposals
Actual:	Approved Proposals (N = 168)	96	72
	Disapproved Proposals (N = 82)	37	45
	Percent Correctly Predicted:	56	
	Correlation Between Discriminant Function and Discriminating Variables:		
	Rule Restrictiveness	.71	
	Agency Type	-.21	
	Department v. Agency	-.13	
	Canonical Correlation	.06	

Table 5.7 Comparison of Approved and Disapproved Agency Proposals in Wisconsin

Committee Action	Restrictiveness	Agency Type	Percent by Departments
Approved (168)	2.79	2.34	68
Disapproved (82)	2.90	2.32	67

Thus, the probability that a Wisconsin legislative committee will object to a regulatory proposal or request modifications is roughly equal for all types of proposals and for all bureaus. There is no indication that the rule review mechanism consistently works to increase or decrease regulatory aggressiveness. Residual analysis was not employed in this case because there was no established pattern from which individual cases could deviate. In short, information on agency characteristics and the content of agency proposals does not help to predict committee action.

Conclusion

There are two reasonable interpretations of the Wisconsin findings: legislative participation in implementation in Wisconsin is intentionally objective, focusing on the legal soundness of administrative proposals without regard for content; or legislative participation in implementation in Wisconsin is regularly influenced by a variety of contrasting interests and is thus explicitly political in each individual application but cumulatively neutral in effect.

Although the discriminant analysis cannot directly resolve the ambiguity, the second interpretation is probably more accurate. In the first place, the narrow "legal" review of administrative regulation is performed by the Legislative Council, and this review is more thorough and meaningful in Wisconsin than in most other states. Any purely legal or technical deficiencies would surely be corrected at that point in the process. Second, legislators would receive no significant benefit from spending time to correct merely legal shortcomings in administrative regulation. It is far more likely that, when they object or request modifications, legislators are acting in response to explicit or threatened political influences.

If this view is correct, the Wisconsin legislative review process must be functionally (as well as legally) open to a fairly representative array of interests, including some proregulatory or public advocate forces. More intensive study would be required to verify such a conclusion, but there are special features of the Wisconsin system that suggest that the "pluralism" hypothesis may, at least currently, be correct for that state.

JCRAR's political position vis-à-vis the regular standing committees fundamentally alters the patterns of influence relevant to legislative participation in implementation. Unlike its counterparts in Michigan and Tennessee, JCRAR has developed into a highly visible, well-staffed overseer, and its broad political support enables it to reject committee disapprovals with little difficulty. Its high profile is due, in part, to the fact that it normally considers only those agency proposals that have caused an impasse between an agency and a committee; it does not perform the routine, generally noncontroversial function that reviewing committees perform in other states. Moreover, the senator serving as cochair through 1982 frequently sought publicity for the committee's actions, specifically those that were supportive of public advocate objectives.[61] Its independence from the regular committees and from regulated interests is apparently guarded carefully by JCRAR's leadership and staff.

Legislators on the regular standing committees are therefore less willing to disapprove administrative proposals in response to complaints that they are burdensome unless the complaints are exceedingly strong (as perhaps in the case of the insurance rule), or unless the agency's proposal is clearly unsound. JCRAR's close relationship with proregulatory forces improves the position of agencies proposing aggressive regulation. The resulting situation is one in which standing committee decisions are based on careful assessments of the influences bearing on each individual proposal. Consequently, the Wisconsin system does not lead to an automatic rejection of proposals opposed by a significant influence, as is nearly the case in the two previously studied states. Disapprovals are determined by the variable level of political support and opposition (as expressed in standing committee hearings and in JCRAR hearings) and are thus not predictable as a function of policy or agency type.

Of course, the fact that formal actions by standing authorization committees are reviewed by JCRAR may simply lead legislators on these committees to work more informally with agencies. Even without final disapproval authority, the authorization committees still have considerable influence (because of their control over agency budgets and enabling legislation), and therefore agency officials probably attempt a compromise when an authorization committee opposes their proposals. If these committees interact informally with agency representatives before regulations are officially proposed, it may be possible that the review process has a greater effect than is revealed by this study.

The insurance and other examples mentioned previously suggest that any such informal effect attributable to authorization committees would be to moderate regulation.

The difficulty of formally disapproving burdensome regulatory proposals may have led legislators to attempt resolution of more substantive regulatory issues through legislation itself. If true, legislative committee rule review in Wisconsin has not led to the separation of policy formulation and implementation that was noted in Michigan and Tennessee. Discussions with staff revealed that, contrary to the reports in Michigan and Tennessee, Wisconsin legislators have not been known to suggest broad delegation when faced with an apparently intractable policy issue while reserving rule review as a way to resolve subsequent conflicts. In fact, there were indications that JCRAR had occasionally taken an active role in suggesting statutory revision.[62]

In short, the Wisconsin experience with legislative rule review appears to be exceptional in several respects. It is, at its best, a truly public-oriented overseer, independent of any single interest or institutional perspective. The most reasonable conclusion that can be drawn is that it is subject to political influence from all directions equally. Legislative participation in implementation may therefore be cumulatively neutral in this setting.

IOWA: EXTREMES OF DECENTRALIZATION

The Process

Legislative committee review of agency regulatory proposals began in Iowa in 1969 with the establishment of the (Joint) Administrative Rules Review Committee (ARRC). Its membership consists of three senators and three representatives appointed by the speakers of each house. ARRC's powers were originally limited to "advising" agencies and recommending legislation relevant to administrative actions, but amendments to its enabling legislation in 1975 and 1978 changed its organizational structure and its power over agency decisions. The 1975 changes gave ARRC a staff and budget separate from the rest of the legislature. Members were given four-year terms "to provide continuity in the rules review process and to allow members time to develop particular expertise in the rule-making process."[63] The

1978 changes created extensive new powers over proposed agency rules, enabling the committee to delay or suspend them.

Iowa also has an administrative rules coordinator, a gubernatorial appointee who independently reviews agency actions and also sits (as an ex-officio member) on ARRC. This office is empowered to prescribe a uniform numbering system for official administrative rules and to "make legal and public policy recommendations to the Governor regarding his power of objection and rescission of any accepted rule."[64]

The typical process for promulgation of new administrative regulations is rather complicated. The agency submits its proposed rules to the coordinator, who reviews them in terms of form and style for publication in the Iowa Administrative Bulletin. After publication, a period of at least 20 days for submission of public comments must expire before an oral administrative hearing can be held. The agency may adopt the final rule after its rule-making hearing by submitting it to the coordinator for publication in the Bulletin as an adopted regulation.

The publication of adopted administrative rules begins a 35-day period for review and objection by both the governor and ARRC. Gubernatorial objection (upon recommendation by the coordinator) takes the form of an executive order and effectively voids the agency decision. Through November 1980, there have been only four instances of gubernatorial objection.

ARRC reviews the agency proposals to determine whether they are "unreasonable, arbitrary, capricious, or otherwise beyond the authority delegated to the agency."[65] The committee may delay the effective date of a proposed regulation or issue a formal objection. Either action requires a two-thirds vote of the committee members. If the first alternative is chosen, the effective date of the proposed rule will be delayed until 45 days into the next regular session of the General Assembly. If the rule is delayed during a session, the delay lasts until the last day of that session, so that the legislature can act on the rule by enacting a joint resolution before it becomes effective.

The delay occasioned by ARRC action can thus be quite substantial. For example, a rule suspended during the summer could be delayed until the General Assembly reconvened in January, a period of some five months. This delay is in addition to the already substantial delay required by the normal rule-making and public participation procedures. Through November 1980, ARRC has suspended six rule submissions, four of which were suspended between legislative sessions.

An ARRC objection does not immediately rescind the agency action, but it does have a legal effect. After the objection is properly certified and filed, the burden of proof in any legal proceeding is placed on the agency to prove that the rule is reasonable. Thus, any person affected by a rule that has met with committee objection can file a suit for a declaratory judgment on the validity of the rule; if the agency fails to meet the burden of proof, the rule must be voided by the court.[66] The purpose of this provision is to encourage and facilitate judicial review of agency regulatory proposals. The committee's action becomes legally influential because the statute defines legislative intent as being indicated by the committee's decision.

Committee objections are also published in the Iowa Administrative Bulletin. Despite the fact that an ARRC objection does not automatically result in annulment of an agency proposal, the publication of the objection and the reversal of the burden of proof certainly can cause problems for the agency. Moreover, ARRC recommends passage of a joint resolution of disapproval whenever it objects to a proposed regulation. If such a joint resolution is passed and signed by the governor, the rule is immediately void.

Since July 1975 ARRC has objected to 155 regulatory proposals, approximately 10 percent of all those submitted to it. Additionally, the committee has referred a number of submissions to other standing committees.

Impact on Agency Decision-Making

The most distinctive characteristic of the Iowa rule review process is the juxtaposition of executive and legislative reviews. Although the two reviews are connected (by staff linkages and by the coordinator's presence on the committee), an agency must satisfy all significant objections that may arise at either review. To assess the administrative impact of the process, it is therefore necessary to determine what kinds of agency decisions are most likely to meet with objection from each source.

According to interviews with the administrative rules coordinator, the staff of ARRC, and a number of agency officials, the initial review by the coordinator focuses upon the "controversiality" of agency proposals. He attempts to prevent adverse action on agency rules (by ARRC and/or by judicial activity) by informally recommending changes when he expects significant opposition to them. The coordinator sees his primary function as preventing political embarrassment to the governor.

The four executive objections to agency rules confirm this impression. They involved a Social Service Department rule governing parental rights in adoption proceedings; a Credit Union Department rule limiting membership in state-approved credit unions; a Chiropractic Examiner Board rule designating a chiropractor as a "physician" for purposes of health insurance coverage; and a Dental Examiners rule prohibiting "attention-getting" signs to designate dental offices.[67] The last three proposals can be reasonably assumed to have aroused opposition from politically significant segments of the public (credit unions, physicians, and dentists), and the first proposal would have undoubtedly aroused generalized public controversy.

The stated reasons for objection in the executive orders are notable in that narrow legal reasoning is usually absent. For example, the Credit Union Department proposal was found unacceptable because it was "an apparently significant deviation from the long-standing legal and public policy of common bonds in credit union membership."[68] The Social Services Department proposal was found unacceptable because it "would impose greater restrictions on children being placed into Iowa from other states than is imposed on children placed intra-state."[69] Legal reasons are occasionally included in support of the objections, but it is apparent that the policy effect of the proposals was the primary impetus to objection.

Of course, it should be recognized that these four objections are simply the only cases in which negotiation between the coordinator and the rule-making agencies broke down. The threat of gubernatorial objection is a real one, and the coordinator can usually inform the agency whenever such an objection is probable. A great number of controversial proposals are modified before final adoption by the agency.

The legislative review takes place subsequent to the coordinator's review, and it typically reflects a different set of concerns. Here, the evidence suggests that agency decisions can be disapproved on the basis of smaller political difficulties and narrow legal arguments. A good example of an objection for relatively minor reasons occurred on March 14, 1979.[70] On this date, the committee objected to a Social Service Department proposal that provided that the state must pay for house repairs costing more than $10 for recipients of Aid to Dependent Children. The committee felt the $10 limit was too low.

A more significant example involved a Revenue Department rule relating to sales taxes on auto repair services performed on autos owned by used car dealers.[71] Several car dealers contended that services they obtained from repair shops constituted "services purchased for resale" since the cars were being repaired so they could be eventually sold to retail customers. According to their line of reasoning, the application of sales tax to these repair services would result in double taxation, since the repairs were being taxed both directly and in the final sale to the person purchasing the car at a higher price as a result of the repairs having been completed.

The committee was unanimously persuaded by the car dealers and issued an objection on September 11, 1978. The Revenue Department refused to alter the substance of the rule. The Iowa Auto Dealers Association then filed suit for a declaratory judgment on the validity of the rule in the Polk County District Court on October 12, 1979, approximately one year after the rule was officially promulgated. The department had decided not to enforce the rule while the litigation was pending.

The court's decision supported the validity of the agency proposal. Although the legal reasoning is not of direct interest to the present study, it should be noted that the case turned on the court's interpretation of the term "ultimate user." The auto dealer obtaining repair services was construed to be the "ultimate user" of the services (thus requiring the application of the sales tax) because the kind of repairs in question are not normally obtained on the direct request of a known purchaser of the car. Tax-exempt repairs would have to be requested by the "ultimate user," and since these repairs are not initiated by a retail customer, the dealer would constitute the "ultimate user" for the purposes of sales tax collection.

This example is typical of a fairly consistent pattern in ARRC objections. The committee generally acts only when significant complaints are brought to its attention and when a case can be made for considering the agency's action unreasonable. In addition to the Revenue rule, committee objections have been filed against proposals that:

> required a minimum of two staff personnel for supervision of juvenile detention in shelter homes;
> prohibited a licensed pharmacist from being employed by a prescriber of prescription drugs;
> required employers to restructure work schedules and to modify equipment so that physically handicapped applicants can be considered;
> required the establishment of a mandatory reporting system prior to the application of certain pesticides;
> required the development of "case plans" for clients in correction centers; and many others.[72]

Of course, most of these objections are linked to legal reasoning. Each begins with the grounds for objection, usually either that the rule is "arbitrary, capricious, or unreasonable," or that it exceeds the statutory authority under which it was promulgated. In some cases, the committee objection is based on the idea that the regulatory change should be made by statutory change rather than by administrative regulation. However, the bulk of the objections cannot be explained purely by reference to legal reasoning.

According to the position articulated in Chapter 3, the kind of committee actions exemplified by the above list is a consequence of the differences between committee hearings and agency hearings as participative opportunities. In this connection, it is interesting to note that the committee staff assistant did in fact feel that the two types of hearings were fundamentally different. Committee hearings were generally quite informal, more like a "town meeting," when compared with agency rule-making hearings. The latter are quite structured and formal, and attendance is usually better. Participants at agency hearings are likely to be members of groups interested in establishing new regulatory systems and programs. The Sierra Club was mentioned as one frequent participant in administrative proceedings, for example.[73] Those participating in the committee hearings are primarily those who object to regulations, usually on the grounds that they are "unreasonably burdensome."

This distinction between the two forums with regard to participation is helpful in understanding typical committee motivations for objections. In legal terms, the committee may object if an agency proposal is found to be "arbitrary or capricious," but it can also evaluate the overall "reasonableness" of the rule. The staff assistant explained that, in practice, this mandate is taken as authority to examine virtually any aspect of a proposal regardless of its consistency with perceived legislative intent. He explained that objections are often made on the basis of what he called "political acceptability."[74]

The committee has developed its own reciprocity norms. The requirement for a two-thirds majority to suspend or object to regulations may be expected to minimize the incidence of frivolous objections. However, there is a strong tendency for the committee to stick together when making objections. If one or two members want to take action against a proposal, the rest of the committee normally goes along.[75] The staff assistant explained that the majority of committee votes are unanimous.

Given this pattern, it is arguable that the existence of the ARRC review affects the broader legislative process. If a review mechanism is available that can defuse any difficulties that may develop after establishment of a new regulatory policy, legislators could be tempted to delegate more broadly to agencies than they would without the mechanism. The committee staff assistant indicated that such a pattern has been observed. He reported that on several occasions legislative stalemates were avoided by a decision not to resolve a difficult policy issue in legislation. One senator reportedly said they should go ahead and let the agency decide the matter because ARRC could monitor their actions.[76] The broader delegation of legislative authority to agencies (and, indirectly, to ARRC) was supposedly one of the reasons for the committee members' four-year terms. "Expertise" in administrative regulation would, it was hoped, be developed, thus making the assembly more comfortable with its broad delegations of power.

The objections evaluated for the study do not provide any clear indication of the connection between legislative intent and committee action. As mentioned earlier, the committee responds to adverse reactions to agency proposals and to its own sense of the objective "reasonableness" and "political acceptability" of those actions. However, its independence from the rest of the legislature does add to the potential for minority coalition influence. In other words, there have been instances in which legislators who had lost a legislative battle over a statutory provision used their influence on the committee to block or moderate agency actions taken to implement the legislation. According to the staff attorney of the Department of Environmental Quality (DEQ), the most notable example of this pattern involved the state law governing disposable beverage containers. The committee objected to a DEQ regulation governing the collection of crushed cans shortly after the statute was enacted. The common interpretation of this action was that disgruntled opponents of the statute were trying to "sabotage" it through ARRC action on the implementing regulations.[77]

Conclusion

A quantitative analysis of committee action was not possible for Iowa because appropriate data were not available. The committee did not keep usable records of all the rule submissions it considered, and thus there was no reliable way to compare approved proposals and disapproved proposals. However, the examples of committee actions discussed above and the interviews with committee and agency staff provide a good basis for assessing the system.

The most consistently reported effect of the rule review process in Iowa was heightened administrative timidity. Agencies still promulgated rules where necessary, and some even openly opposed committee action (the Revenue Department, for example). However, the prospect of delay and difficult litigation leads Iowa administrators to try to avoid committee displeasure whenever possible. The addition of the administrative rules coordinator's executive review makes agencies especially tentative when considering rules that are potentially controversial.

It should be noted, however, that any antiregulatory impact of the legislative review process cannot be attributed to an explicit ideological stance by committee members. The committee is very similar to its counterparts in Michigan and Tennessee in this regard. It is not a haven of libertarian or antibureaucratic political sentiments. Instead, it simply responds to the inputs it receives, typically objecting to onerous regulatory restrictions and requirements.

Executive involvement does not appear to act effectively as a centralizing force. One agency member suggested that the coordinator's presence on the committee was usually important, but that he did not often act as an advocate for the agencies. Since the coordinator performs an initial review of agency proposals, it is likely that he serves as a mediary between the agency and the legislators on the committee. He is in a position to report on this analysis of the rules in question, but he apparently does not often attempt to prevent committee action when it has a real interest in objecting to agency rules.

The political structure of the implementation process in Iowa has thus been additionally fragmented as a result of its system of legislative and executive review of agency regulation. Agencies must satisfy several largely independent reviews of their decisions, and committee action even expands and encourages judicial review. It is thus possible for a very small political force or an individual legislator to block (or threaten to block) agency action.

As in the other states, legislative review in Iowa does not constitute a careful, extensive policy evaluation of agency action. The staff of ARRC consists of only two persons, a generalist administrative coordinator (working on a law degree at the time of this study) and a secretary. In most cases, the assistant merely drafts the legal justifications for committee objection. He does not act as an instigator for objection, even in the narrow legal sense in which his Michigan counterparts do.

In the long run, the advent of a more extensive legislative role may require that stronger political coalitions be formed in order to establish and effectively implement many kinds of regulatory policy. Where such coalitions are formed administrative effectiveness may be ultimately improved; the same political influences that are generated for the purpose of averting legislative blockages may also be helpful in maintaining general support for the agency's program. Compliance may be improved where regulatory policies have successfully cleared all the reviewing hurdles. However, the cases examined here suggest that legislative review can easily delay implementation when broad-based political support is not sufficient. It is reasonable to assume that, in addition to these delays, legislative participation has a chilling effect on administrators contemplating difficult regulatory action. Consequently, the nearly unanimous opposition to ARRC on the part of Iowa administrators is not difficult to comprehend.[78]

GEORGIA: THE IMPORTANCE OF THE INFORMAL

The Process

Provision for legislative review of proposed administrative regulations was included in the 1977 amendments to the Georgia Administrative Procedure Act.[79] As in many other states, the reform was publicly advocated as a way to correct bureaucratic irresponsibility and to reduce the extent and cost of regulation.

Agencies are now required to send copies of proposed regulations to the legislative counsel at the same time that they give formal notice of an intent to adopt new rules, amendments, or repeals. The counsel performs a simple review of the rules with regard to writing style and the agency's statutory authority. The rules are then sent, on behalf of the presiding officers of both houses, to the appropriate standing committees.

The committees may or may not consider the proposals at this point. If a committee decides to examine them, it can hold hearings and negotiate with agency officials. A formal objection may occur if these negotiations reach an impasse, in which case a letter of objection is filed with the agency. If the agency refuses to change the proposal, a bill may be introduced which, if passed by a two-thirds majority of each house, results in an immediate veto of the proposal in question. A positive vote of less than two-thirds must be signed by the governor before the rules are affected.[80]

The most striking characteristic of the Georgia legislative review process is that it does not create any new formal powers. No new committee with special jurisdiction over agency rule-making is established. Legislative review of agency decisions takes place through the same process that exists for other legislative actions. As of November 1980, no rules had been voided by legislative enactment, and only five committee objections had been filed. (In all but one of these cases, the agency capitulated to committee objections.)

Impact on Agency Decision-Making

The administrative process has not been fundamentally altered as a result of legislative participation in agency rule-making. The vast majority of administrative decisions pass through procedures which, as in most other states, facilitate a minimal amount of citizen involvement and public awareness. Without special structures or staff devoted to review of agency rule-making, legislative participation is intermittent at best. The new law itself establishes no legislative powers over agencies not already available; the legislature was always empowered to prohibit or amend most agency actions by normal legislative enactment. Under normal conditions, the new system merely requires that agencies make additional copies of their rule submissions so that they can be submitted to the legislative counsel.

In the absence of a special reviewing structure, legislative participation in administrative decision-making takes place through the same standing committees that control agency budgets and enabling statutes. The expectation that legislative review could act as a counterweight to subsystem relationships thus does not apply in Georgia. Agencies are not required to work with a new set of legislators who have an independent institutional perspective. Their regulatory proposals are reviewed by the same committees that have authority over other agency activities and agency budgets.

The fact that patterns of authority and linkage are not changed by the new law may explain the extremely low incidence of objections. One would not expect that Georgia agencies have been markedly less active than those in the four states previously studied. The unusually low number of objections is more likely a function of the fact that there is no new pattern of influence operating in the implementation process.

If anything, the new provisions simply increase the legitimacy of legislative participation in regulatory policy implementation. The standing committees receive copies of proposed rules and realize that they are empowered to review them. As a result, agency rules probably receive more legislative scrutiny now than they did before the new provisions were enacted. Substantive committees may be more willing to suggest changes in agency rules since they now review them before they are proposed. Under the old system, any rules considered by the substantive committees would be reviewed only after they became effective; thus, the agency could resist legislative objections by arguing they would require significant changes in operations. Many minor legislative objections were probably abandoned as a result. Under the new system, legislators are probably more willing to press for changes.

Even this limited review process is apparently causing some changes in legislative-administrative relations. As noted in other states, the availability of legislative review may have prompted Georgia legislators to delegate broader authority to administrators. A staff assistant on the House Health and Ecology Committee reported that his committee frequently decided to let the boards or agencies under its jurisdiction resolve some issues by regulation that could not be resolved by the committee. He explained that "we can always review what the board comes up with" when the implementing regulations are promulgated.[81]

In this connection, it is interesting to note that the number of rule promulgations is noticeably lower during the legislative session than when the legislators are not in session. An assistant to the legislative counsel, whose office originally noticed this trend, suggested that agencies were attempting to avoid legislative scrutiny by timing their rule submissions to occur in the late summer or fall. Of course, most of the committees can and do hold meetings during the period between sessions, making this strategy only partially effective.

Documentary data were obtained on three of the committee objections that had occurred through November 1980. Each objection had been made by the House Health and Ecology Committee, which normally receives nearly two-thirds of all Georgia's administrative regulations. They will be examined in some detail because the legislative and administrative motivations involved help to explain the impact of the review on agency decisions. The substantive effect of the committee actions led, in all cases, to moderation of the force, scope, or impact of the agency proposals.

One of the first actions taken under the new review procedures was an objection to a proposal of the Georgia

Board of Nursing filed in September 1977. The Health and Ecology Committee objected to a single line of that board's proposed amendments, one that would have prohibited the issuance of temporary permits to applicants waiting to take (or retake) the examination to become registered nurses.

The Board of Nursing explained the rationale for the prohibition of temporary licensing in an undated memorandum submitted to the Health and Ecology Committee. It was pointed out that persons with temporary certificates are often employed with no supervision and that most of these persons "have not yet demonstrated possession of minimum knowledge for the practice of Nursing."[82] Moreover, it is allegedly difficult to know when a temporary permit expires (because the expiration date is different for each applicant), and thus, many persons with temporary certificates continue working after they are no longer licensed. The board concluded that its "obligation of accountability to the Georgia public" required it to prohibit temporary licensing.

The formal objection by the committee did not contain any statement of reasons. However, a member of the legislative counsel staff surmised that some hospitals would find it difficult to obtain adequate staff support if the regulation became law. These interests reportedly influenced the committee to file an objection. The board capitulated and the proposal was withdrawn.

The second case involved a large set of regulations dealing with ambulance services. The Department of Human Resources had promulgated proposed rules in January 1979 regulating several aspects of ambulance design and the qualifications of drivers. The committee objected to eight provisions: a provision defining the term "invalid car" to exclude cars used for emergency purposes; a provision requiring ambulance personnel to wear a patch identifying them as licensed personnel; a provision requiring ambulance personnel to successfully complete the Georgia emergency medical technicians course and to hold a current CPR card; a provision requiring that each ambulance be manned by at least two certified emergency medical technicians while transporting an emergency patient; a provision requiring that each ambulance be stocked with several safety and first-aid items; a provision requiring that all ambulances involved in major accidents be reinspected and approved by authorized ambulance builders; a provision designating the proper operating frequency for ambulance radios; and a provision authorizing the Department of Human Services to inspect the premises, records, and personnel files of persons providing ambulance services.[83]

The Health and Ecology Committee directed one of its subcommittees to investigate the proposed rules. Its report, submitted on February 13, 1979, recommended that the committee object to the eight provisions noted above. The subcommittee argued that one of the provisions might conflict with a statutory definition, and that another did not adequately standardize ambulance operations. The other six were disapproved because they would "place an unnecessary burden" on ambulance personnel or ambulance service providers.[84] This aspect of the regulations was clearly the most important to the subcommittee, as it concluded in its summary that "provider input has been largely ignored in the development of the proposed rules and regulations."[85] The department reconsidered and agreed to modify the provisions.

The final example involved a regulation proposed by the Georgia State Board of Nursing Home Administrators. The legislature had passed a statute in 1980 that stated that "two years of experience working in a nursing home shall be equivalent to one year of any academic education and training requirements established by the board" relating to standards for license as a nursing home administrator.[86] According to an administrator in the Georgia secretary of state's office (which has administrative jurisdiction over all Georgia licensing boards), the board interpreted the term "experience" to mean "experience in a management level position." The board's regulation reflected this interpretation, requiring that experience to count as education must be in positions such as "assistant administrator, director of nurses, or business office manager." The rationale for the regulation was the board's opinion that experience as a gardener at a nursing home should not be counted against the education requirement for nursing home administrators.[87]

The Health and Ecology Committee objected to the regulation because it "exceeded the board's statutory authority." Certainly the committee had a cogent legal argument; the effect of the regulation was to limit the kind of experience that could be counted against academic requirements, and no direct authority was delegated to the board to enact such a limitation. On the other hand, this kind of interpretation is not uncommon in administrative regulation, and many contend that it is quite proper. The objection led to a modification of the rule by the board, and no limitation on experience is in effect as of this writing.[88]

Conclusion

Officials in two agencies, the legislative counsel staff, and legislative committee staff explained that legislative participation in policy implementation in Georgia is normally limited and predictable. A committee is most likely to act when a regulated organization, usually a licensed profession, disagrees with regulations proposed by the board or agency authorized to regulate it. As noted earlier, regulated groups usually have considerable influence in the decisions of these boards, and thus, it should not be surprising that legislative actions in response to complaints (by regulated groups) about the activities of licensing boards are rare.

It is perhaps puzzling that committee objections have resulted in agency modifications in nearly all cases in light of the fact that the committees have no formal power to act independently. If an agency does not want to alter its original proposal, the committee objection cannot block the agency action unless it is approved by a two-thirds majority of both houses or is passed by the legislature and signed by the governor. Many objections made by committees would not, one would assume, be upheld by legislative enactment. Whatever power the committees have must therefore have an informal foundation.

The fact that the committees reviewing official administrative proposals also recommend legislation and budget changes for the same agencies is the most likely explanation for their apparent power in implementation decisions. Administrators normally depend on the substantive committee with jurisdiction over them for political support, as scores of studies have shown.[89] Giving these committees the opportunity to review proposed agency rules expands their influence over the agencies even if the opportunity to review is not accompanied by formal or legal powers.

The normal patterns of authority and influence in legislative-administrative relations are thus strengthened by the Georgia system. It can be argued that the policy subsystems made up of agencies, legislative committees, and interest groups in a common policy area are made more cohesive and autonomous as a result of the new legislative review process. It reinforces agency dependence on committee action, a dependence presumably rather strong in the first place. When the bureau considers stepping outside the limits of subsystem interests (as perhaps the Nursing Board did in response to a legitimate concern for the public safety problems associated with temporary licensing), legislative participation can be invoked to reassert a subsystem perspective. Of course, the access opportunity is available to any interest, but the normal relationship between committees and agencies suggests that the committees will be more receptive to influence by clientele groups than by public advocates or unaffiliated citizens.

It is striking that, in Georgia, the objections involved proposals from occupational licensing boards, the same kind of agencies that were particularly unlikely to meet with legislative objection in Michigan and Tennessee. Moreover, there were no environmental or work-safety regulatory proposals disapproved in Georgia, again a surprising result in light of the high incidence of objections to those kinds of proposals in Michigan, Iowa, and Tennessee. Since there is no reason to assume that Georgia's legislators are simply more sympathetic to environmental and work-safety programs than their counterparts in other states, there must be some fundamental or structural difference that accounts for the absence of objections to these kinds of agency proposals. While many explanations are tenable, it is possible that environmental agencies and OSHA-type agencies are less likely to develop subsystems than occupational licensing boards, and that legislative participation within the Georgia structure only comes into play as an extension of subsystem politics. Environmental standards are debated and influenced through traditional committee and legislative processes.

This explanation suggests that the substantive committees are prone to use their reviewing powers only on those rare occasions in which an agency normally responsive to subsystem interests advocates policies opposed by the subsystem or at least by parts of it. Environmental regulations are not made within the same kind of narrow subsystem relationship. Different influence strategies are apparently used when they are opposed. A manufacturing group may eschew an appearance before an environmental authorization committee reviewing proposals for new pollution standards, and instead decide to press its interests before other committees or before the whole assembly. Such groups may be more successful in Georgia in their efforts to block enabling legislation for these kinds of regulatory programs. However, a nurses association (in close contact with the nursing board and the committee with jurisdiction over nursing) may find it quite agreeable to press for committee action on the rare nursing board rules it opposes. A joint committee charged to review the reasonableness of all government regulations would provide an access point more accessible to those opposing regulations from outside the subsystems. Since this is absent in Georgia, the kinds of objection prevalent in the other states do not occur.

The relatively low number of committee objections supports the idea that generally cooperative patterns of legislative-administrative relations are not notably altered by the presence of legislative review. The absence of an independent committee with its own staff precludes the possibility that legislative participation will engender a comprehensive, systematic evaluation of agency policy. There is also no institutional basis for a reviewing process that magnifies the importance of generalized complaints regarding regulation, as in Michigan and Tennessee. Instead, the Georgia experience reveals what happens when a new mechanism of legislative participation is introduced into an existing setting without changing authority patterns: the simple reinforcement of subsystem politics.

NOTES

1. For a particularly one-sided view, see John H. Sheridan, "Can Congress Control the Regulators?" Industry Week, Vol. 188 (March 29, 1976), pp. 20-27. A good, but narrow, legal analysis is provided in George Bunn and Jeff Gallagher, "Legislative Committee Review of Administrative Rules in Wisconsin," Wisconsin Law Review, Vol. 1977 (1977), pp. 935-988.

2. Glendon Schubert, "Legislative Adjudication of Administrative Legislation," Journal of Public Law, Vol. 7 (1958), pp. 135-161.

3. Ibid., p. 161.

4. William Lyons and Larry W. Thomas, "Legislative Oversight: Legislator Attitudes and Behavior in Three States," paper prepared for delivery at the Annual Meeting of the Midwest Political Science Association, Chicago, April 18-21, 1979.

5. Ibid., p. 16.

6. Keith E. Hamm and Roby D. Robertson, "New Methods of State Legislative Oversight: A Comparative Analysis of Adoption and Implementation," paper prepared for delivery at the Annual Meeting of the American Political Science Association, Washington, August 31-September 3, 1979.

7. Ibid., pp. 27-33.

8. The index of innovation is described and analyzed in Jack L. Walker, "Innovation in State Politics," in Politics in the American States, 2d ed., Herbert Jacob and Kenneth Vines, eds. (Boston: Little, Brown, 1971), pp. 354-387.

9. See Marcus E. Ethridge, "Regulatory Policy Administration and Agency-Citizen Linkages in Southern States: Some Hypotheses and an Exploratory Analysis," in Contemporary Southern Political Attitudes and Behavior, Lawrence Moreland, Tod Baker, and Robert Steed, eds. (New York: Praeger, 1982), pp. 268-285.

10. Ethridge, "Legislative-Administrative Interaction as 'Intrusive Access': An Empirical Analysis," Journal of Politics, Vol. 43 (May 1981), pp. 473-492.

11. Ibid., pp. 487-489.

12. Ibid. For a more detailed investigation of the policy consequences of the procedural reforms, see Ethridge, "The Policy Impact of Citizen Participation Procedures: A Comparative State Study," American Politics Quarterly, Vol. 10 (October 1982), pp. 489-509.

13. It should be noted, however, that some attempt was made to "control" for this factor in the analysis. See Ethridge, "Legislative-Administrative Interaction," pp. 488-489.

14. Information on the Elazar-Sharkansky political culture scale can be found in Ira Sharkansky, "The Utility of Elazar's Political Culture," Polity, Vol. 2 (Fall 1969), pp. 66-83; for the innovation scores, see Walker, p. 358.

15. (Michigan) Joint Committee on Administrative Rules, "Processing of Proposed Guidelines and Administrative Rules," pamphlet published May 1979.

16. Tennessee and Wisconsin, among several other states, allow this procedure.

17. Michigan Compiled Laws, Section 24.241 (2).

18. Michigan Joint Committee on Administrative Rules, p. 2.

19. Interview with Nick Bosen of the Michigan DNR, October 1980.

20. Ibid.

21. Interview with Bruce Andrews, Michigan Office of Secretary of State, October 1980. This item was also reported in the Detroit News, September 25, 1980, p. 19-A.

22. Interview with Terrence Bronson, staff attorney of the Michigan Joint Committee on Administrative Rules, October 1980.

23. Interview with Bosen, October 1980.

24. Interview with Bronson, October 1980.

25. The terms "rule submissions" and "agency proposals" are used to designate the unit of analysis because the records were constructed on the basis of sets of rules rather than individual rules. Since there is no standard length for a rule, a rule submission constitutes a more consistent unit of analysis. It should also be noted that submissions or proposals include amendments or repeals as well as new regulations.

26. It could be argued that this position predicts that agencies most likely to be subsystem partners (regulatory agencies) will be relatively immune to legislative disapprovals, and that committees will be led to focus their attention on agencies promoting "protective regulatory policy." However, it is possible that even subsystem partners may be forced (by public advocates) to propose burdensome regulations against the subsystem interests. Thus, if committee action occurs as predicted by this position, most if not all agencies should encounter some committee objections, although typical objections would be designed to protect regulated or client groups.

27. Some classifications were made after briefly examining proposed rules by the agencies.

28. There were a few proposals (five) that were coded 1 and 4 by the coders. These proposals were usually cases in which it was not possible to determine whether the agency action was purely symbolic or actually restrictive (for example, the dedication of a wildlife area). These cases were considered uncodable and were omitted from the analysis.

A standard index of intercoder reliability, pi, was computed for the data on rule restrictiveness. According to Holsti, this approach to measuring reliability is sensitive to both the number of possible categories and "the probable frequency with which each is used." Pi can be computed as follows:

$$\text{pi} = \frac{\%\ \text{observed agreement} - \%\ \text{expected agreement}}{1 - \%\ \text{expected agreement}}$$

The expected agreement is the sum of the squared proportions of the items falling into the categories (as determined by a sample coding). Using this formula, the reliability of the data on restrictiveness was .43.

While this level of agreement is acceptable, some content analyses have achieved higher levels. However, most analyses obtaining substantially higher reliability scores are those employing simple factual categories. Holsti points out that some reliability must often be sacrificed when dealing with complex concepts; the results may be more useful despite the lower reliability of the coding. See Ole R. Holsti, Content Analysis for the Social Sciences and Humanities (Reading, Mass.: Addison-Wesley, 1969), pp. 140-142. Greater reliability could undoubtedly have been obtained here if the coders scored regulatory proposals by length or some other clear criterion, but the connection between such an indicator and the issue at hand would be tenuous.

In evaluating the reliability of the data, it should be noted that: the results were computed separately on the basis of each coder's decisions to check for coder bias, and the same general results were obtained independently with both sets of data; and while the coders assigned identical scores in 60 percent of the cases, their disagreements were over adjacent categories in an additional 30 percent. Consequently, the coding process indicated that an identifiable dimension exists in the data set.

29. It is likely that the bulk of committee influence is exerted informally and that the relatively rare formal objections only occur when a compromise is not possible. According to several interviews, agencies typically attempt to modify their proposals in accordance with the Joint Committee's requests.

30. The results clearly show that there is considerable overlap in the predicted groups of agency proposals, but the discrimination on the basis of the discriminant function is, nonetheless, statistically significant.

31. These boards included all those that regulate a specified profession or occupation. An umbrella department coordinates the boards and provides centralized clerical support.

32. Acts of Tennessee General Assembly, 1975, chapter 370, Sections 20-21.

33. This conflict produced an emotional display from the controversial Governor Blanton, but it also led to an interesting legal opinion from the state attorney-general, dated December 22, 1975.

34. For a detailed analysis of this episode, see R. Craig Williamson, "Legislative Review of Administrative Rules and Regulations: A Review of American State Legislatures and a Case Study of Tennessee's General Assembly," M.A. Thesis, University of Tennessee, December 1980.

35. Ibid.

36. Williamson, pp. 82-83.

37. Tennessee Code Annotated, Section 4-510 (h).

38. Williamson, p. 71.

39. Interview with William N. Bates, director of the Administrative Procedures Division of the Office of Secretary of State, Tennessee, April 1980.

40. The rules in question were Alcoholic Beverage Commission Rules 0100-1-01 through 0100-3-06.

41. The opinion was written by Assistant Attorney-General William C. Koch, Jr., and was released on March 7, 1977.

42. Interview with officials of the Alcoholic Beverage Commission, April 1980.

43. Of course, opponents of the legalization of price advertising argued that such a change would be contrary to public interests because, among other problems, the advertisements could increase liquor consumption. Astonishingly, the liquor retailers' association reportedly made this argument. Their real motivations were sufficiently transparent to most observers.

44. See Williamson, p. 91.

45. The disapproval was voted in April 1980. See Williamson, pp. 94-95.

46. Ibid., pp. 93-94.

47. Ibid., ch. IV.

48. The same index of intercoder reliability computed for the Michigan data was employed here. A slightly higher figure was obtained (.46). As with the Michigan data, nearly all of the cases of coder disagreement were over adjacent categories.

49. Williamson's conclusions are on pp. 117-119.

50. Ibid., p. 118.

51. Interview with David Berger, former Senate co-chair of JCRAR, August 1981. Also see JCRAR, Annual Report: 1979-1980, pamphlet, January 1981, pp. 1-3.

52. State of Wisconsin ex rel. Wisconsin's Environmental Decade, Inc. v. JCRAR, et al., 73 Wis. 2d 234 (1976).

53. Letter, dated July 12, 1979, obtained from David Berger, August 1981.

54. JCRAR, Biennial Report: 1979-1980, p. 13.

55. Ibid., pp. 15-16.

56. Reported in the Capital Times (Madison, Wisconsin), August 10, 1981, p. 5.

57. The committee action was reported in the Bulletin of the Proceedings of the Wisconsin Legislature, 1981 Session, Supplement, p. 8.

58. Interview with David Berger, August 1981.

59. Ibid.

60. Computation of pi, the index of intercoder reliability, resulted in a score of .52, a bit higher than for Michigan and Tennessee. Again, of the 34 percent of the cases in which the coders did not assign identical scores, most were disagreements over adjacent categories.

61. Interview with David Berger, August 1981.

62. Ibid.

63. Joseph Royce, "The Rules Review Process in Iowa," mimeo., dated October 1979, p. 13.

64. (Iowa) House of Representatives Information Office, "Iowa Administrative Rules Guide," Iowa State Printing Division, Des Moines, April 1980, p. 3.

65. Code of Iowa, Section 17A.4, 4.a.

66. Code of Iowa, Section 17A.4, 4.a. and 4.b.

67. State of Iowa Executive Department, Administrative Rules Executive Orders: Number 3, November 6, 1979; Number 1, October 9, 1979; Number 2, October 9, 1979; and Number 4, November 23, 1979.

68. Administrative Rules Executive Order, Number 1.

69. Administrative Rules Executive Order, Number 3.

70. Notice to Iowa Department of Social Services from Iowa Administrative Rules Review Committee of the General Assembly, March 14, 1979.

71. The Revenue Rule in question was Rule 26.2(6). The department began the process of amending it in June 1978. The following information is from documentary records and an interview with Carl Castelda, deputy director of the Iowa Department of Revenue, October 20, 1980.

72. These examples are drawn from documents and other information acquired in an interview with Joseph Royce, staff assistant for the Iowa Administrative Rules Review Committee, October 20, 1980.

73. Interview with Joseph Royce, October 20, 1980.

74. Ibid.

75. Ibid.

76. Ibid.

77. Interview with Department of Environmental Quality officials, October 20, 1980.

78. Both the Revenue Department and the Environmental Quality officials reported that such opposition was common.

79. Georgia Code Annotated, Section 3A-104 (e) (f).

80. Ibid.

81. Interview with William Miller, legislative assistant, Health and Ecology Committee, Georgia House of Representatives, November 1980.

82. Undated memo from Georgia Board of Nursing to the Health and Ecology Committee of the Georgia House of Representatives.

83. Notice of objection sent by Health and Ecology Committee, Georgia House of Representatives, February 15, 1979.

84. Recommendations of the Health and Ecology Subcommittee on Proposed Rules and Regulations for Ambulance Services, February 13, 1979.

85. Ibid., p. 4.

86. Georgia Code Annotated, Section 84-4903 (d), quoted in memo from Representative Eleanor Richardson and Representative Tommy Smith to the Health and Ecology Committee, August 1, 1980.

87. Interview with Michael Fowler, Office of Georgia Secretary of State, Licensing Boards Division, November 1980.

88. Notice of objection sent to chairman of the Georgia State Board of Nursing Home Administrators, from Health and Ecology Committee, August 13, 1980.

89. J. Leiper Freeman, The Political Process: Executive Bureau--Legislative Committee Relations, rev. ed. (New York: Random House, 1965); Ira Sharkansky, "An Appropriations Subcommittee and Its Client Agencies," American Political Science Review, Vol. 59 (September 1965), pp. 622-628; and George Goodwin, Jr., The Little Legislatures (Amherst: University of Massachusetts Press, 1970).

6

A SYNTHESIS OF THE STATE EXPERIENCES

The empirical investigation of legislative participation in implementation presented in the previous chapter indicates that while each experience is unique, certain general conclusions are possible. Since the scope of this research is restricted to five states, however, the conclusions should be taken as empirically based propositions for further inquiry and not as final answers. Generalizing from the data and the impressions in the case studies, the following propositions appear tenable.

PROPOSITION I

Legislative Committee Review of Formal Agency Proposals Constitutes a De Novo Review of Implementation Decisions

The most common justification given for the new forms of legislative involvement in agency decisions is the maintenance of legislative intent in implementation. As noted earlier, proponents of legislative review mechanisms point to cases in which agencies adopted provisions from defeated bills in their own rule-making. Legislative surveillance is advocated as a logical way to prevent and correct this kind of contradiction of legislative intent. It is considered natural and proper for committees to be the instrument of this legislative check because the scope of the review is allegedly limited to a neutral evaluation of whether the agency action is faithful to legislative intent as previously expressed by the whole assembly. In other words, much of the rationale underlying these mechanisms implies that the review will not constitute a thoroughgoing reevaluation (by a single committee) of the practicality, desirability, or political value of policy decisions, but that it will be limited much as judicial review of agency action is limited. The unrepresentative nature of the reviewing structure is legitimized by virtue of the narrowness of its scope of review.

The state studies do reveal instances in which legislative participation approximates the narrow, technical-legal review some have perhaps envisioned. Most notably, the Michigan Joint Committee on Administrative Rules routinely objects to agency decisions that are, in a legal sense, vague and open-ended. There were cases in Iowa in which similar issues were raised when objections were filed. Moreover, reports of the Florida experience (discussed briefly below) suggest that legislative review in that state, supported by an extensive staff of attorneys, has resulted in an enormous improvement in the legal soundness of formal agency decisions and in the consistency between legislative intent and agency rules.

Despite these important cases, however, the bulk of the evidence indicates that legislative committee involvement in implementation decisions normally constitutes a functionally unlimited review of any and all aspects of agency action. Of course, to some extent, the broad scope of legislative review is inevitable because of the ambiguity of applicable statutes. Empowering committees to determine whether agency actions are consistent with legislative intent unavoidably constitutes a blanket authorization to evaluate any aspect of an agency decision considered important because it is almost never clear how legislative intent relates to a given administrative action. Thus, committee members are free to designate virtually any action they dislike as improper on this basis. Where statutes add that the committee can object to agency actions considered "unreasonable" or "arbitrary," in addition to those found contrary to legislative intent, it is obvious that legislators are not constrained by a narrow legal mandate.

More important, legislative participation in implementation does not focus on narrow, legal issues because that kind of approach is inconsistent with typical legislative orientations. Legislator perspectives are dominated by concerns for constituency interests and bargaining where policy decisions are at stake. Legislators have routinely used formal powers over such technical matters as rules for debate to obstruct certain policy decisions. It would be unrealistic indeed to expect them to perform a narrow, "judicial" evaluation of agency adherence to legislative intent simply because that is their formal function.

The extent to which this kind of legislative participation constitutes a de novo review of agency action is a question centrally relevant to an assessment of the new legislative role. Much of the theoretical support for committee review of agency proposals for new regulations rests on the assumption that the committee will not displace the law-making power of the whole legislature. This is assured only as long as the scope of the review is meaningfully limited. The broad review observed in the states studied here suggests that some kind of displacement has occurred.

Moreover, the de novo character of the review performed by these committees suggests that their actions are possibly subject to the same problems of arbitrariness that have led to the elimination of most de novo reviews of administrative action by courts. It is well-established in administrative law that an unlimited review introduces new opportunities for arbitrary action, and judicial review is therefore normally limited to a review of procedural regularity and statutory authority.[1] To the extent that committee review of formal agency decisions is effectively unlimited, political influences in the reviewing process become more important, and these influences may not be supportive of the influences acting on the whole assembly during policy formulation.

This proposition presents a direct challenge to Lowi's assumptions regarding the reestablishment of legislative authority. Although it is still possible that a new legislative presence in implementation could moderate subsystem influences even when the legislators are not explicitly motivated to guard legislative intent (as discussed in Chapter 2), the empirical evidence presented in Chapter 5 makes it difficult to support Lowi's position. Clearly, it cannot be easily assumed that statutory purposes will be upheld in implementation simply because legislators are given new formal powers.

PROPOSITION II

Legislative Participation in Implementation Focuses upon Those Aspects of Agency Decisions that are Opposed by Regulated or Client Interests

The most consistent finding in the five state studies was the special vulnerability to legislative objection of agency policies that add to the regulatory burden. Legislative review did not routinely address fiscal changes or moral concerns raised by agency actions. Distributive policies, such as grants of assistance to eligible recipients, were also relatively immune to legislative objection. Even restrictions creating a burden on those attempting to enter a regulated profession (usually proposed by occupational licensing boards) were rarely the subject of legislative committee opposition. However, when new prohibitions or requirements were applied to regulated interests, legislative objection was quite likely.

The quantitative analysis of agency decisions in Michigan and Tennessee revealed this finding most clearly, establishing that disapproved agency proposals scored significantly higher on restrictiveness than the approved proposals. No other characteristic on which data were available was useful in distinguishing between approved and disapproved rules. Moreover, when the occupational licensing boards were omitted from the analysis, the relationship between restrictiveness and the probability of disapproval became considerably stronger. Since licensing boards often propose restrictive rules actively sought by the regulated, this result adds further support to the proposition that committee objections are disproportionately directed toward agency proposals that are opposed by the regulated. The qualitative analysis of all five states adds support to this general conclusion.

In Michigan the lobby-registration regulations proposed by the Secretary of State provide a good example of this pattern of legislative objection. The proposed regulations would have required expenditure disclosures that were opposed by nearly all lobbyists. The Wisconsin authorization committees with jurisdiction over insurance policies objected to a regulation that would have established upper limits for some kinds of credit life insurance premiums. The Iowa Joint Committee objected to a Revenue rule that would have (and eventually did) levy sales taxes on auto repairs performed for used car dealers. A Georgia authorization committee objected to a variety of rules establishing minimum requirements for ambulance equipment. The Tennessee reviewing committee objected to a rule limiting services performed by hearing aid dispensers' assistants, and it objected to a rule that would have allowed advertising of retail liquor prices. The consistent factor in all of these cases is the high probability that the regulated groups involved opposed the agency actions. The empirical evidence, both quantitative and impressionistic, suggests that this is the most likely precondition for legislative committee action.

Thus, the findings indicate that legislative participation in implementation does not affect all types of administrative decision-making equally. The prevailing wisdom regarding legislative motivations and capacities suggests that legislators, even with enormous expansions of staff and research resources, are not able to evaluate all administrative decisions in any detail. Some method for selection must be developed to guide legislative review. Political pressures coupled with limited legislative capacities create a situation in which legislative participation focuses disproportionately upon agency decisions that generate effective opposition from identifiable, salient, and usually regulated interests.

PROPOSITION III

Legislative Committees Established to Review Agency Regulations Develop Institutional Perspectives to Legitimize Their Actions

Whenever an organization must operate in an uncertain and potentially conflictual political environment, there is always a danger that its efforts will be impeded by opposition from organizations with competing interests. An oversight committee is particularly likely to encounter significant opposition because its general jurisdiction overlaps the jurisdictions of other committees, most notably the authorization committees. This difficulty is generally cited as a primary reason for the ineffectiveness of the Congressional Government Operations Committees as oversight agents.[2]

Of course, the rule review committees studied here (those in Iowa, Michigan, Tennessee, and JCRAR in Wisconsin) have a clearly identifiable function, making it difficult for them to avoid conflict with authorization committees through a strategy of inaction. The simple avoidance of authoritative action (resulting in unquestioned approval each month of scores of administrative proposals) would be uncomfortably conspicuous. Thus, rule review committees must produce tangible results, both because of their formal position and in response to the political pressures discussed in Chapter 1.

These committees must develop some base of legitimacy to counter the inevitable political opposition caused by their authoritative actions. The development of an overt, widely recognized institutional perspective is one way of achieving this. If public pronouncements and modes of operation can be designed so that the committee will be perceived as acting predictably and in accordance with accepted political values, the committee can establish itself in the larger committee system. An effective institutional perspective makes the committee <u>appear</u> to be approaching agency decisions from a special, limited frame of reference, thus avoiding the allegations that it is substituting its judgment for that of the authorization committees or the whole assembly.

One approach to creating institutional legitimacy is to assume the role of a "grievance appeals board." Both the Michigan and Tennessee review committees effectively pursued such a strategy by assuming a public profile of a committee with special concern for groups and individuals whose needs and interests have been ignored by agency decision-makers. Most of their disapprovals were publicly defended not on the basis of substantive analysis, but as necessary responses to insensitive, myopic bureaucratic actions. The records of agency rule-making hearings, indicating the frequency and magnitude of unresolved complaints about agency proposals, were thus more important for committee decision-making than an analysis of substantive problems.

This emphasis on grievance appeals enables the committees to operate, with tangible results, without independent examination of policy questions, thereby reducing conflict with other committees. Official objections do not imply that the reviewing committee is making a claim for the jurisdiction of the authorization committee that oversees the agency in question; it implies only that the administrators involved had not given sufficient attention to public concerns. The role of a grievance appeals board thus creates the impression that the review is a limited one and, by referencing committee decisions to mainstream values of democratic responsibility, the reviewing process is accorded a strong measure of legitimacy.

The Wisconsin JCRAR and, to a lesser extent, the Iowa ARRC took a slightly different approach to defining their place in their respective committee systems. These committees acted as "even-handed referees" by emphasizing the political neutrality of their actions. Thus, review decisions were not automatically defended as necessary responses to bureaucratic insensitivity. These committees act in a more overtly political manner, pursuing a more difficult strategy that requires careful management in order to preserve the perception that they are not providing an access opportunity for only a special type of influence.

Structural variations help to explain the choice of this mode of operating. The Wisconsin committee generally reviews only those agency proposals that have resulted in authorization committee objections. Its position is thus formally that of a "referee" between agencies and authorization committees. The Michigan and Tennessee committees hear complaints about agency decisions from interest groups and individual citizens, making it natural for them to operate under an announced assumption that agencies need to be more responsive to public complaints and problems. The fact that the Wisconsin JCRAR reviews only well-defined conflicts between agencies and committees precludes such an approach. Instead, it must consciously steer a neutral course, nurturing the perception that neither committees nor agencies automatically prevail.[3]

The Iowa ARRC sometimes acts very like the Michigan and Tennessee committees, but explicit political neutrality is a greater concern in its actions. This is primarily because of the presence of the governor's administrative rules coordinator on the ARRC itself. As an official representative of the governor, he presents the executive position on agency proposals, providing a political point of reference not usually present in the other states' reviewing operations. Rule review in Iowa thus becomes a focal point of legislative-executive interaction, making certain committee decisions directly relevant to broader political concerns. Consequently, the Iowa ARRC frequently attempts to balance its decisions so that it is perceived as neither a rubber stamp for the governor nor his constant adversary.

There is another type of effective institutional perspective, although it has not been adopted as the primary role of any of the committees studied here. It is possible for a committee to assume the role of a "strict legal guardian" by reviewing only the narrow question of statutory authority. Given a political interest interpretation of the origin of legislative participation in implementation, one would expect that this kind of review process would be rare, and indeed, there is only one committee currently in existence that has reportedly operated in this manner.

Florida's Joint Administrative Procedures Committee issues an annual report of its official activities in which all of its decisions are noted and explained. If this report is an accurate account, the Florida committee acts almost exclusively to police agency adherence to legislative intent. All of the objections are described as being necessary because the agency in question had exceeded a specific, identified element of its statutory authority.[4] While perhaps many of the objections are arguable, they are all supported by solid legal reasoning showing that the agency involved had not been authorized to issue the restriction or interpretation included in its proposals.

Performing this kind of legislative oversight requires a large, expert legal staff, so it is not surprising that the Florida committee has a larger staff than any of those studied here. The committee employs five full-time attorneys, two legislative analysts (one with a law degree), three secretaries, and a part-time student, in addition to an executive director. The staff carefully examines all agency proposals for possible violations, and its recommendations are nearly always acted upon by the committee.[5]

This kind of institutional role probably produces the greatest protection against intercommittee conflict, but it makes legislative participation less flexible. When it becomes established that all committee objections are justified on the basis of narrow legal issues, legislators are hesitant to recommend objection to legally proper proposals that are allegedly unsound or because of a belief that the agency should compromise more earnestly. The restriction of legislator prerogatives, coupled with the substantial staff requirements of such a system, help to account for the rarity of this approach despite its effectiveness in protecting the reviewing committee from allegations of arbitrariness and political favoritism.

If an institutional perspective helps oversight committees to become established in the larger committee system, it is likely that such a perspective may also help to shape the policy impact of their oversight activities. Assuming the role of a grievance appeals board probably magnifies any tendencies for a reviewing committee to moderate policy, since it lends special legitimacy to disapprovals based on perceptions that administrators are overly aggressive. The even-handed referee role leads a committee to support several different interests, and thus, it probably tends to weaken any decidedly pro- or antiregulatory consequences. The Florida system was not studied here, but a cursory review of some of the activities of its Joint Administrative Procedures Committee suggests that its policy effects may be as distinctive as its staff support. A substantial proportion of its objections appear to be directed toward occupational licensing boards that allegedly exceeded statutory authority in their efforts to restrict entry into licensed professions.[6] If this is normally a major thrust of the Florida reviewing system, its policy implications are strikingly unlike those observed elsewhere, particularly in Michigan and Tennessee. Table 6.1 is a summary presentation of the likely differences among the kinds of institutional perspectives discussed here.

Table 6.1 Institutional Perspectives of Oversight Committees and Their Basic Characteristics

	Staff	Legal Powers	Spur to Action	Policy Effects
Grievance Appeals Board	Small	Broad	Salient complaints about agency action	Decreased regulatory aggressiveness
Strict Legal Guardian	Large	Narrow	Staff report on statutory authority	Reduces anti-competitive regulation
Even-Handed Referee	Small	Broad	Changing balance of support and opposition	Neutral

PROPOSITION IV

The Volume and Nature of Legislative Participation in Implementation Is Affected by the Reviewing Unit's Structural Independence from Existing Policy Subsystems

The legislative review systems studied here represent different alternatives in terms of their structural relationship to the other committees: joint committee with authority to review administrative regulations (Iowa, Michigan, and Tennessee); authority to review given to authorization committees (Georgia); and authority to review given to authorization committees with final power to act given to a joint committee (Wisconsin). The structural variation was important in determining how the review process worked.

The most extensive and distinctive legislative participation was observed in Iowa, Michigan, and Tennessee. Since committees in these states were established primarily for review of administrative actions, it should not be surprising that they engaged in this activity with some regularity. If nothing else, these committees must justify their existence and role, and this requires some significant level of formal output.

These committees' structural independence from authorization committees is the feature that makes them attractive to many reformers who advocate oversight power as a way to counteract subsystem politics. The experiences of Iowa, Michigan, and Tennessee suggest, however, that the most important consequence of structural independence may be the elimination of a substantive focus in oversight activities. Perhaps as a result of legislative norms regarding respect for committee jurisdictions, these special reviewing committees were conspicuously interested in limiting the scope of their inquiry. Instead of an in-depth analysis of the substance of agency proposals, members of these independent committees asked merely "How many complained at the hearing?" or "Were public concerns adequately handled?" Legislators did not often ask for supporting studies or data relevant to an administrative proposal. While some of this reticence about substantive analysis may be due to limitations on staff and other resources, it appears that the structural independence itself may indirectly inhibit the kind of careful substantive analysis usually thought to be a central feature of effective oversight. As discussed above, these committees instead work to create an institutional perspective that explicitly limits their involvement in the substantive aspects of implementation decisions.

Georgia's system did not involve the establishment of any new structure, and its operation was quite different from the others. The effects of legislative participation under this system were merely an extension of typical legislative-administrative relations where subsystem politics controls. No influence patterns were created to challenge normal subsystem relationships between authorization committees and agencies. Consequently, legislative action on agency rules was infrequent and always intended to support the positions presumably favored by the subsystem interests.

The Wisconsin system constitutes a hybrid design in a structural sense. Initial review authority is in the hands of authorization committees, but final action on their objections is the responsibility of the joint committee. The initial review process is, not surprisingly, similar to that in Georgia--there were few formal objections, and most of these were in the direction of moderating regulatory policy. Since most legislative dissatisfaction with agency rule-making does not result in formal objections but only leads to requests for changes, it is likely that legislative participation in this state normally supports subsystem preferences.

However, when agencies prove recalcitrant to authorization committee preferences, a formal objection is made, which is then sent to JCRAR for its concurrence. Because of the nature of its political support, there is no guarantee that it will support authorization committee objections; indeed, JCRAR appears pleased with its record of independence from authorization committee influences. This two-tiered structure thus presents an interesting decisional situation for agencies. If administrators are not willing to change their proposals in face of authorization committee opposition, they know there may be a good chance of having a favorable hearing in a subsequent JCRAR review of the authorization committee's objection. When the issue in question is of sufficient importance, administrators may refuse to make changes and hope for a favorable resolution when the matter goes to JCRAR.

If this interpretation is accurate, the Wisconsin system dilutes the power of the subsystems, but does not eliminate it. Agencies still want to avoid incurring the displeasure of the substantive committees that have jurisdiction over their affairs. The fact that there were many more "requests for modifications" than formal objections indicates that, in most cases, agencies capitulated to the authorization committees when legislative opposition surfaced.

A rough comparison of these cases suggests that there is a salient qualitative difference between interest group influence within subsystems and interest group influence with agencies and committees outside their subsystems. Legislative participation in the states in which a structurally distinct mechanism performs the initial review (Iowa, Michigan, and Tennessee) occurred most frequently when interests were subject to regulation from agencies outside their subsystems. For example, general contractor companies were much more likely to use the joint reviewing committees in these states to oppose proposals by the Department of Natural Resources than to oppose the few they did not favor by the General Contractors Board. The rare occasions in which occupational licensing boards were the subject of committee disapprovals in these states occurred when these boards proposed changes at the behest of public advocates (for example, the Alcoholic Beverage Commission rule in Tennessee).

When legislative participation initially occurs through authorization committees (Georgia and Wisconsin), a very different set of influences apparently develops. Since environmental, equal opportunity, and work safety regulations are reviewed by authorization committees ostensibly committed to these policies, opponents of these regulations do not have a structurally independent access point to which they can voice complaints. These regulatory programs are therefore debated through more traditional lobbying processes. Legislative review in these states is, however, well-designed for responding to complaints from regulated or client groups about regulatory proposals made by their erstwhile subsystem partners (for example, the insurance rule in Wisconsin and the nursing rule in Georgia).

The idea that subsystem linkages are a distinctive form of influence is a critical part of the argument advanced in Chapter 2. In simple terms, the progressive reformers advocating legislative participation in implementation assume that structural changes can be made that counteract subsystem linkages while augmenting other types of influence that presumably represent broader values. The research reported here adds support to the idea that subsystem politics does exist, but it appears that a review process independent of subsystem politics does not necessarily lead to decisions contrary to subsystem interests. In fact, it can be argued that where independent review mechanisms are not directly supervised by higher political actors (such as the administrative rules coordinator in Iowa or JCRAR in Wisconsin), these mechanisms may become part of an antiregulatory subsystem made up of interests and legislators generally opposed to aggressive regulation. Structural independence from subsystems should not be expected to facilitate public-spirited regulation.

PROPOSITION V

Legislative Participation in Implementation Leads to Broader Delegation of Policy-Making Authority from Legislatures to Administrators

The idea that delegation of legislative authority is accelerated as a consequence of the growth of the new review mechanisms is difficult to prove. It is clear that the breadth of delegation is due to many factors, and the importance of a greater legislative role in implementation in this connection is open to question. However, the state experiences observed here provide some support for this idea.

The consistency with which committee staff noted the "delegation effect" was striking. Someone in nearly every state mentioned that legislators had referred to the possibility of subsequent committee review of agency decisions when arguing that a particular issue should be delegated. Many of these delegations would have occurred with or without the review mechanisms, of course, but such statements indicate that they probably had some effect. In fact, it appears that a formal legislative presence in implementation legitimizes broader delegation because it makes it possible for legislators to delegate without really removing themselves from the decisional process. As they become more institutionalized and established, it is likely that the legitimizing effect of such mechanisms will become even more important.[7]

A summary analysis of the main findings makes it clear that there is considerable variation among the approaches to legislative review of formal agency action, and other states may be assumed to have adopted still different approaches. However, the similarities among the three states with initial review by joint reviewing committees--both with respect to their official orientations and the substantive impact of their actions--indicate that some important generalizations can be derived from the analysis. The concluding chapter discusses the relevance of these generalizations to broader evaluations of the effectiveness and the representativeness of the policy process.

NOTES

1. A good but controversial statement of this principle can be found in a recent Supreme Court decision. See Vermont Yankee Nuclear Power Corp. v. Natural Resources Defense Council, Inc., et al., 435 U.S. 519 (1978).

2. Lawrence C. Dodd and Richard L. Schott, Congress and the Administrative State (New York: Wiley, 1979), pp. 167-193.

3. The former Senate cochair of JCRAR, David Berger, related one episode in which he actually told an authorization committee meeting with an agency representative that they "could not leave the hearing room until some compromise is reached." More typical applications of JCRAR's referee role are undoubtedly more subtle.

4. (Florida) Joint Administrative Procedures Committee, Annual Reports (1975-1980), mimeo., Florida Legislature.

5. Reported in testimony of C. Curtis Kiser, Florida House of Representatives, before the Administrative Practice and Procedure Subcommittee of the Senate Judiciary Committee, U.S. Senate, September 13, 1978.

6. For example, in 1981 the committee objected to a rule that would have required commercial, wholesale, or retail live marine species dealers to pay a $25 application-processing fee. The committee stated that "none of the statutes cited as law authorize the Department to charge a processing fee of $25.00." Joint Administrative Procedures Committee, Annual Report, January 1, 1981 to December 31, 1981, mimeo., n.d., p. 18.

7. Louis Fisher, "A Political Context for Legislative Vetoes," Political Science Quarterly, Vol. 93 (1978), p. 250.

7

CONCLUSIONS: THE NEW LEGISLATIVE ROLE AND DILEMMAS OF REPRESENTATIVENESS

It is perhaps now a commonplace observation that the basic nature of political conflict has changed in the United States. Whether referred to as "postindustrial society," the "age of reassessment," or a "new pluralism," it is often argued that a new policy process has evolved, one in which new interests press in different ways for new kinds of values.[1] A basic idea of this book is that the new legislative role in implementation is itself a part of these changes. When recent alterations of legislative influence are interpreted without reference to these broader social and political changes, analysts reach generally unsatisfying conclusions about a legislative "resurgence."

The purpose of this final chapter is to draw together the concepts that best explain recent developments in legislative-administrative relations and the empirical evidence regarding the policy consequences of new legislative powers. Consideration of these broader problems reveals that the origins and effects of the new legislative presence in implementation transcend the immediate, practical concerns of public administration and have direct implications for larger questions about U.S. political institutions.

HAS THE POLITICAL ENVIRONMENT REALLY CHANGED?

In Chapter 1 it was argued that the emergence of effective public advocate groups disrupted policy subsystems by effectively opposing previously unopposed interests in the implementation stages of the policy process. Strong incentives for legislators to participate in implementation decisions are a likely consequence of this disruption. However, if these groups are largely similar to other types of interests, it is arguable that the current changes are merely a temporary process of adjustment, and that public advocates will eventually develop effective linkages to friendly bureaus just as other groups have. Legislative participation in implementation will once again become inhibited as new subsystems develop and demand ever-increasing autonomy.

Yet, there are reasons to expect that the changes caused by public advocacy are not temporary but are part of a basic transformation of pluralist politics. The new public advocate groups are arguably quite different from the groups normally involved in the classic subsystem syndrome. Mancur Olson's reasoning is instructive here in his suggestion that there may be significant qualitative differences between "noneconomic" groups and "the main economic pressure-group organizations" to which his theories most directly apply.[2] Noneconomic groups, roughly equivalent to public advocate lobbies as the term is used here, are characterized by "rich and obscure" relationships between individual and group interests, making them generally inscrutable in terms of a rational theory of collective action.

If true, Olson's reasoning implies that noneconomic groups are unlikely to develop the kinds of subsystems that normally inhibit a strong legislative presence in implementation. If these organizations press for general values and collective goods that do not "selectively benefit the membership or activists of the organization," then it will be difficult or impossible to respond to their demands through the kinds of policy decisions most common in policy subsystems: distributive policy and regulatory policy protecting a regulated interest from competition.[3] In short, the groups do not form for the purpose of satisfying the selective needs of their members, and thus, subsystem politics cannot easily serve their interests.[4]

Along with the emergence of a new type of political organization, a special variety of public policy has become increasingly important in recent years; in fact, the new interests and policies are closely associated. Ripley and Franklin contend that what they call "protective regulatory policy"--exemplified by pollution controls, consumer protection requirements, and other restrictions advocated by public interest groups--is very different from "distributive" policy or "competitive regulatory" policy:

> many of the interactions during the implementation of protective regulatory policy will be characterized by hostility which is specific rather than abstract. The interactions are also cast in adversarial terms because the restricted clients do not get rewards, rather they receive directions, punishments, or constraints upon their actions. This policy area is activist in that implementers must take positive steps to implement. . . . the affected interests [the regulated] prefer non-implementation and will certainly not take the lead in stimulating implementation.[5]

If protective regulatory policy and noneconomic groups have assumed increasing prominence in the contemporary policy process, it is reasonable to conclude that an important transformation has taken place in the patterns of political conflict. Observations by several analysts representing quite different perspectives confirm this idea. For example, the "new public administration," a movement beginning in the late 1960s, was itself an indication of the institutional changes being wrought by expanding public advocacy and new public policies. According to the supporters of new public administration, the proper administrative role should no longer be one of passively accepting policy formulations from elected officials. The new administrator should mobilize political activists who advocate the kinds of policy decisions not adequately supported by elected officials: environmental protection, equal opportunity requirements, and redistributive programs.[6] Most analysts and practitioners of public administration are not willing to adopt these suggestions as a wholesale replacement for the traditional administrative values of accountability and efficiency, but the fact that the movement exists at all indicates that institutional roles may be changing. At least some administrative officials apparently feel that they should assume a proactive role, joining forces with progressive public interest organizations.[7] Wherever administrators behave in accordance with these new public administration principles, the policy process is sure to become more conflictual, making legislative-administrative relations increasingly controversial.

Writing exclusively about environmental policy, Lynton Caldwell argues that compromise is becoming inappropriate for resolution of policy conflicts. Unlike distributive or competitive regulatory policy, environmental policy allegedly has a special tendency to create zero-sum conflicts; environmental values cannot, we are told, be compromised.[8] Caldwell's reasoning raises important questions about the ability of institutional arrangements to make and implement this kind of policy effectively.

More generally, Lawrence Dodd, in a provocative essay on Congress, contends that the "preoccupations of the sixties and seventies" have acquired legitimacy and increased salience, altering "the structure of political conflict."[9] Established coalitions that had usually achieved some success in subsystem arrangements were challenged by new forces and were torn from within by the new issues. Traditional patterns of influence have largely become supplanted by new and more conflictual patterns.

The structural changes instituted to facilitate legislative participation may be interpreted as the primary systemic adjustment associated with these changes in the policy process. The "new pluralism" of public advocate groups and traditional interests making incompatible demands about new kinds of implementation problems cannot be accommodated within the traditional institutional arrangements that were previously the structural underpinnings of subsystem politics. The impact of these structural changes is an important empirical question.

Ironically, a stronger legislative role in implementation may appear to be a reasonable and necessary response to the disintegrative forces operating in the policy process; it is often seen as a way to reestablish central public authority. Some legal analysts, and those who oppose delegation of authority on political grounds, have in fact interpreted the stronger legislative role in such a positive manner. However, while much political rhetoric supports this interpretation, actual experience suggests that the new control mechanisms do not make a legislature capable of bringing large public purposes to bear on implementation questions.

The reason that these structural alterations do not achieve a general reassertion of legislative power is not that they have been designed poorly or that they have been sabotaged by judicial or executive decisions. The best explanation has to do with a fundamental characteristic of legislative power as it has been designed on both the state and national levels: the inability to assert an institutional will. Dodd explains how legislative power was deliberately fragmented by constitutional design because of a fear, quite understandable in the agrarian society of the late 1700s, that legislative power could come to dominate all governmental affairs.[10] While the structure created a workable balance for a time, the increasingly complex and urbanizing society eventually led to overly fragmented legislative institutions. The structural features designed to prevent legislative dominance ensured a fundamental weakening of the institutional will of the legislative branch.

THE PARADOX OF THE NEW LEGISLATIVE PRESENCE IN IMPLEMENTATION

When new legal powers over administrators are introduced into such a structure, the absence of an institutional will makes it unlikely that they will lead to a strengthening of legislative mandates. Thus, while the emergence of the new legislative role in implementation may have been caused by the increasing power of public advocacy and the increasing importance of difficult varieties of public policy, the new role is unlikely to reverse the problems of fragmentation engendered by these changes in the contemporary political environment. Additional formal powers wielded by legislatures with weak institutional wills may actually exacerbate the problems that, according to some accounts, led to their adoption.

Of course, concluding that legislative participation in implementation is unlikely to reassert a "legislative will" does not imply that the new mechanisms have no effect; the research reported here has been designed to assess the nature and extent of the policy consequences of a basic variety of legislative participation. The general finding that, absent special structural conditions, regulated groups are probably the greatest beneficiaries of committee rule review, confirms the expectations of some analysts who view such reforms as destructive of administrative planning capacity and neutral competence. However, the theory that best accounts for the finding, augmented by observation, suggests that any antiregulatory effect is the result of differences in the strengths and influence strategies of public advocates as compared with those of regulated or client groups. While there is perhaps a tendency for legislative participation in implementation to benefit the latter groups disproportionately, it is possible that public advocates will use the mechanisms more effectively in the future. A simplistic view of legislative controls as inherently antiregulatory must be discounted, despite the fact that the mechanisms have, so far, not been cumulatively neutral in their effects.

The more fundamental concern has to do with the continuing and possibly advancing separation of policy formulation and implementation. The mechanisms are utilized because legislators leave significant, controversial details to be determined in implementation; while this may allow certain legislators to profit politically by responding to the complaints that surface after administrative resolution of these details, such responses do not create a coherent policy process. As Fiorina explains, the achievement of coherence in legislative influence would require some way of "making the fate of individual members more dependent on institutional performance and less dependent on their personal efforts."[11] It is clear that legislative committee rule review mechanisms, for example, do not achieve any such change in incentives. If anything, they make it possible for legislators to profit from their personal efforts more effectively. They should not be expected to minimize the problems of "liberal democracy."

RECOMMENDATIONS

It would be unsatisfying indeed to have advanced a thesis based on the assumption that political incentives persistently shape legislative action and then to recommend changes that are impossible as long as those incentives operate. Consequently, no realistic recommendations can be made that will be expected to correct the basic problems of fragmentation in the U.S. political system or even those in legislatures. Only a fundamental change in constitutional arrangements creating new electoral systems and legislative-executive relationships could have such a result, and these changes could have other effects making them unacceptable.[12]

However, there are a few recommendations that address the possible harms associated with the development of the mechanisms studied here. Since they are within the capabilities of the present structure, they should be considered by those contemplating adoption of new approaches to legislative participation in implementation.

First, when power to review and suspend administrative proposals is given to legislators, the power should be given to a joint committee with jurisdiction over all agencies rather than the existing standing committees in each house. The Wisconsin system reveals that such a committee, with the proper leadership and in a context with strong public advocates, can act more flexibly than regular substantive committees. The Georgia experience indicates that legislative participation in the latter kind of system will not only be intermittent, but will also be directed toward strengthening subsystem interests where broad values intrude.

Second, the joint committee with formal powers over agency regulations should be subject to the procedural requirements governing notice, publicity, and public participation in administrative rule-making proceedings. Hearings before these committees would be more complex than those before other committees, but the procedural change would help to maintain the continuity of influences as implementation moves from agencies to the reviewing legislators. This reform would directly address the concerns expressed in Chapter 3 regarding the lower visibility and hence lower representativeness of the legislative review. Moreover, requiring the formal trappings of administrative rule-making in these legislative deliberations could make the mechanisms more acceptable in terms of constitutionality.

Third, the official reasons for suspending or disapproving agency decisions should be formally expressed and published (in the same publication that provides official notice of agency rule-making) whenever such actions are taken by a committee. It is well established that the requirement of a statement of reasons is good protection against arbitrariness by administrators when making formal or informal decisions.[13] It is anomalous to allow these decisions so carefully protected against arbitrariness to be suspended or disapproved with no statement of reasons.

Such a requirement would provide some deterrence against wholly unfounded committee decisions (although it is clear that some "reasons" can be formulated to rationalize almost any decision). It would also lead to some degree of consistency in committee decisions since the published reasons for them would inevitably serve as precedents.

Fourth, steps should be taken to make it clear that decisions subject to committee review are not final until committee review is completed. The publicity requirements suggested above should have this effect, but where there are any doubts statutes should unambiguously indicate that the rule-making process is not finished until committee approval has been obtained. Establishing this fact in the law would make it clear to all those with a stake in the final outcome of a regulatory decision that their participation must be effective throughout the process if it is to have any lasting impact.

Finally, committee decisions approving agency actions should be made by majority vote, not by concurring majorities of both the House and Senate members. The latter system, as implemented in Michigan, makes agency decisions subject to very small coalitions, creating the possibility that agency actions can be blocked by the preferences of one or two legislators. While this situation already occurs outside the context of committee review of agency action, its likelihood is increased when approval of agency action requires concurrent majorities of both the House and Senate members of a joint committee.

Perhaps more clearly than anything else, a study of legislative participation in implementation demonstrates that political representation is a complex, even a paradoxical concept. Not all forms of legislative influence are equally valid with respect to democratic principles, even when legislative influence is exerted on unelected bureaucrats. In the absence of an acceptable definition of the "public interest," we can only conclude that different interests are represented by different government institutions, bureaucratic or legislative in character. The most important issue is not private versus public interest, but how to construct institutional arrangements so that interests are represented in a manner conducive to fair and effective government. The research reported here does not provide an easy answer. However, an empirically based understanding of the policy consequences of various approaches to legislative control is surely the best foundation for constructive reform.

NOTES

1. See Lawrence C. Dodd, "Congress, the Constitution, and the Crisis of Legitimation," in Congress Reconsidered, 2d ed., Dodd and Bruce I. Oppenheimer, eds. (Washington, D.C.: Congressional Quarterly Press, 1981), pp. 390-420.

2. Mancur Olson, Jr., The Logic of Collective Action, rev. ed. (New York: Schocken, 1971), pp. 159-165.

3. Jeffrey M. Berry, Lobbying for the People (Princeton: Princeton University Press, 1977), p. 7.

4. The distinctiveness of the new type of political demands is discussed in Lynton Caldwell's analysis of environmental values as a "new factor in public policy." See Lynton Caldwell, Environment: A Challenge for Modern Society (Garden City, N.Y.: Natural History Press, 1970), pp. 20-26.

5. Randall B. Ripley and Grace A. Franklin, Bureaucracy and Policy Implementation (Homewood, Ill.: Dorsey, 1982), pp. 132-133.

6. See Frank Marini, ed., Toward a New Public Administration (Scranton: Chandler Publishing, 1971).

7. William L. Morrow, Public Administration, 2d ed. (New York: Random House, 1980), p. 354.

8. Lynton Caldwell, "Responsibility and Responsiveness: The Anomalous Problem of the Environment," in People vs. Government, Leroy Rieselbach, ed. (Bloomington: University of Indiana Press, 1975), pp. 300-327.

9. Dodd, p. 400.

10. Ibid., pp. 390-394.

11. Morris Fiorina, "Congressional Control of the Bureaucracy: A Mismatch of Incentives and Capabilities," in Congress Reconsidered, 2d ed., Lawrence Dodd and Bruce Oppenheimer, eds. (Washington, D.C.: Congressional Quarterly Press, 1981), p. 345.

12. Ibid., p. 344.

13. Kenneth C. Davis, Administrative Law and Government, 2d ed. (St. Paul: West, 1975), ch. 13.

INDEX

ABOUT THE AUTHOR

MARCUS E. ETHRIDGE (Ph.D., Vanderbilt University) is currently Associate Professor of Political Science at the University of Wisconsin, Milwaukee. He is primarily interested in the policy consequences of changes in American governmental institutions, particularly those affecting legislative behavior. He has published his research in the *Journal of Politics*, *Polity*, *Legislative Studies Quarterly*, and *American Politics Quarterly*, among other journals.